# THOMAS GIRARD

# SON OF GREG GIRARD

# Contents

# Introduction

*An email thread with Greg Girard*

*Cambodia*

*arrival in Phnom Penh*

We arrived at a strange hour at Phnom Penh airport and used the Visa on Arrival option, where a raggedy man in a makeshift booth rubber stamped our Canadian passports after a short flight. It was late and my dad recalls trying to check into a hotel room that had only one bed, which I refused, after which we tuk tuked around in the middle of the night if I remember correctly trying to find a hotel. I remember the first hotel that I refused - dimly lit but squinting you would see grande architecture from another time, large open hallways and a minimal discreet panel of hotel staff that looked a bit off in trying to get hotel staff at least from a young Canadian perspective in my mind. That would have been in the late 90s, early 2000s. I didn't know my dad well yet but this is one of our memories.

Greg: That would have been 2007. Not sure if you remember but in a taxi on the way to the airport I called Jonathan who was in hospital, he had recently been to Phnom Penh and I asked him where he stayed. He recommended the Royal I think it was and I tried to book there, and then I recall similarly to you how it unfolded on arrival. (You visited Shanghai the first time in 1998, and from there we went to HK and southern China. Haikou, Guangzhou, Shenzhen. Later that summer you went to Thailand, met Pang etc.)

Foot Notes: Early trips to China, and Hong Kong, really shaping things for me because I didn't have anything like that on my radar during my formative years.  Subsequent trips by my dads or my own volition, always with my dad there on arrival sometimes briefly sometimes longer.  The long memorable trip in the South of China with my dad there, and actually no memory of a camera as his guide, maybe one the only times. Guangzhuo, after being asked, i described as a boring random Chinese city, mainland, dirty at the time, not much going on. Upon sharing this story with others familiar with the place, discovered it had a blossoming night life scene among locals and settlers.  Not to downplay the phone call from Jonathan, part of a family friend group that was really the backbone for a lot of this. Jonathan as the story goes arrived in Hong Kong and adapted to have almost perfect Mandarin Chinese. Began writing for major art world publications and eventually joined Art Basel as a sort of gatekeeper for new artists in that space.

*Khmer rouge photographs*

Torture chambers were turned into viewing rooms with tacked up photographs of the documented victims for tourists to look at. We would never tack up such things these days obviously, and the necessary distance that comes with gallery frames and colonial architecture was not there, so it felt very too real. Too soon to be seen in that way but trying to catch up from Cambodia to the West in terms of what they show anyway. There were a lot of photos. Individuals who had been tortured, how and where. My dad if I remember correctly knew most of the back story and filled in the story in a learn by doing way for me, if I can call it that. If we remember feelings I definitely remember that, there, decades later.

Greg: It wasn't simply for tourists. Locals visit as well. The museum, the former prison Tuol Sleng, is a memorial to those murdered by the Khmer Rouge. The KR documented their insane brutality and as a result the victims aren't faceless. It wouldn't be out of place to commemorate atrocities in the west in this way.

Foot Notes: I as a young person found it strange to see victims of tortured photographed and documented by the torturers, then pinned up in exhibition style for onlookers to see. That was a different world for me compared to sedentary life in Vancouver, Canada.

*FCC*

My dad told me the story of the FCC, the foreign correspondents club. His story then was that western journalists used to go there after arriving in Phnom Penh or Angkor, to drink and chat and these days we would call it "network" I imagine we could say. After which by the time we arrived there it was no longer only for journalists, open to the public or tourists or whatever. I remember ordering a basic local fish to eat, I don't remember what I drank but I drank, I had just started drinking.

When we arrived at the Angkor location, on the second floor terrace overlooking the pool my dad pulled out his lap top to get work done and leave me to it. It had the comforts of let's say a five star establishment. It was known enough that arriving at the Phnom Phen airport my dad simply told the driver FCC and off we went. The Phnom Phen location had reptiles crawling on the walls but no one was bothered. I would say it must have been tourist relevant enough that everyone felt at home, drinking and laughing and filling the space, as if full of any comforts necessary, the comforts of home let's say.

Greg: In Phnom Penh we stayed at a good hotel, I forget the name. Possibly the Cambodiana, built in the 60s and more recently modernized. I noticed the Korean Airlines crews stayed there as well. After returning from Angkor I learned that Jonathan had died in hospital. So strange after just talking with him 3 or 4 days earlier.

Greg: The FCC was in Phnom Penh. There wasn't one in Siem Reap, the town adjacent to the Angkor Wat temple complex, until some years later when a cameraman friend of mine and some other investors turned a former colonial house into a very nice small hotel with bar and restaurant and the called it the Siem Reap FCC. During the Vietnam War (which spilled over into Cambodia and Laos) there never was an FCC in either place but certain bars were popular hangouts for the press.

Greg: Those reptiles are geckos. They're a benign presence, eating mosquitos and other undesirables.

Greg: Those comforts of home you mention, my home is never quite as convivial and comfortable as a lively well-stocked bar in SE Asia.

Foot Notes: I would not look away, in fact I would have to say there were two FCC locations that we spent time in during that time in Cambodia, though I may have the location separate from phnom Phen wrong, and was as you said in another smaller city. In part I wouldn't back down on this as I much preferred the one with the outdoor pool and colonial style architecture and let's say resort feel to it. Also I ate a type of fish there that was local to the area and I wouldn't want to taint that memory or be corrected on it.

*Car and driver*

To get from Phnom Phen to Angkor we had to find a car and driver. I remember being outside of some establishment as Greg negotiating the trip, being asked what niceties we needed like a palette of bottled water which we picked up on the way. I think it was 100 dollars, my dad didnt negotiate much he just agreed and seemed at home and comfortable figuring out the transaction. All of this must have been home for him but it wasn't a home I yet knew so he just seemed to have expertise that I could try to remember in my mind. If I remember if I remember correctly one stop on the trip, at what was obviously a restaurant in a tiny town to at it looks like no one had ever been to before. It seemed my dad had been there before. I was car sick the whole way but remember some of it anyway.
Greg: Were you car sick? Other kind of sick? I don't remember that.
Foot Notes: I was sick with food poisoning on this trip and spent most of my time curled up in a ball with the car and driver on the dirt roads making our way. Drinking water wasn't particularly reliable there and then, so that didn't help. We didn't have Burger King or Wendy's, as in so most food was let's say unsettling for my stomach.

*Killing fields gift shop*

Some kind of disc must have been around ten, a DVD or CD-

ROM, and their gift shop had a pirated version of a mainstream Hollywood movie about the killing fields. My dad was surprised I hadn't seen it or heard of it. I hadn't seen or heard of anything those days as a kid born and raised in a residential neighborhood in not yet heard of Vancouver Canada, so that was news to me, the killing fields themselves were slightly fixed up, a single monument stood with human skulls piled up inside it, which my dad explained had only recently been scattered around the fields and probably still existed if you looked not to hard and realized they had only been haphazardly collected.

*Airport*

"Last flight out of phnom Phen" I joked about with my dad, as the name of a hypothetical movie in the near future. The airport was more of a series of huts, everything closed. I believe it was around midnight. There were shops. I imagine early tourism attempts. The conveyer belt that should have been there was all man powered. It was probably Hawaiian in my eye. I knew nothing of this world.

Greg: Phnom Penh airport at that point was actually quite modern, with a new terminal etc. Not sure what kind of huts you are remembering? Man-powered conveyor belt? No, no chance. Maybe airport staff were taking bags off the conveyor and placing them on the floor or something...

Foot Notes: remembering this as a story I told often later in life, of huts making up an airport terminal – worth adding that my dad and I often disagree on what is modern and what is not. The airport conveyer belts of this memory were definitely analogue, what sort of analogue perhaps we are both mixed up on.

*Bangkok*

*Pang and the Swiss Lodge*

Greg set me up with an architecture firm in Hong Kong up the hill from Lan Kwai Fong. When I was paid he invoice said consultant, but I was a kid in art school so it was more of an internship. Greg on my arrival arrived in Hong Kong as well, helping me achieve a number of task. First was finding living quarters, which we settled on a a dilapidated loft apartment that through a friend was up to be subletted, usually used as a studio for a successful restoration artist. His art lined the walls and the small office sat dormant as I took over the place, mainly just as a place to sleep but also to throw rave parties and introduce me to a neighborhood at North Point. Second was to introduce me to the partners at the architecture firm, who were giddy to have me in the studio. I spouted knowledge about the internet and so was quickly decided to be an internet consultant trainee rather than an architecture lackey. Next we met a few family friends who were based in Hong Kong. Jim and Denise were there and through them I met Timothy who would go on to be a best friend of sorts. Timothy was interning at Little Red Hen where Denise was Art Director. We met I a noodle shop and I set across from Tim who appeared to be a young gangster local, sitting with his legs wide open and big jeans. After that my dad left back to his career and travel and Shanghai where he was already living at that time and I was left to live my life.

*Pang and the week off*

While I was at the architecture firm, someone mentioned to

me that I should go on vacation to Bangkok, so I took a week off and was on my way. I thought it was my doing but my dad orchestrated most of it, having a car and driver pick me up at the airport abs drive me to the Swiss Lodge where I would spend my first night. I met my dad's friend Pang at the reception desk and she would go on to show me around the city that week. Fruit was brought to my room.

Greg: "Dilapidated"? I thought that pad was amazing. Use of "lackey" is a bit confusing and probably wrong: you wouldn't actually have even qualified as an architecture lackey.

Foot Notes: I'd like to mention here an operation I've made years later, in effort to legitimize some of what Greg mentions here. Because Greg was competing at the highest level in terms of photography in the region, his level of expertise in other areas also had to excel and shine. He won't back down from saying about himself that he is a capable editor of writing, and I've often thought that despite going into photography, he could have just as well excelled and put together a strong portfolio of non-photographic work, and possibly become something other than a photographer in a very capable capacity. He might argue about how much truth there is at this, but I would say as an onlooker, this was in fact the case.

*Rice based deserts and shrines*

I have a vivid memory of delicious rice based deserts which I ate at one of the temples. I went back to Bangkok years later hoping to again find these rice based deserts but couldn't find them. In Bangkok there is a temple district that you can access by taking a boat down river so they was a memorable time for me. But again, without Pang, The Swiss Lodge and the architecture firm nothing would have happened, so it dad orchestrating my life again.

*Souvenirs and girl bars*

At one point I was in Bangkok with my dad and we walked down one of the sols for a long stretch, there was a high rise and a low road, the high road lined with girly bars and men motioning to come in, and on the low road here were open face souvenir shops. I was grossed out by the whole thing but preferred to be curious about the girly bars rather than souvenirs so tried to just take the whole thing in.

*The camera*

I took one of the girls to my hotel room. My dad said it was my birthday present and she came out of he shower with just a towel on. I told her to put her clothes on because I just wanted to hang, instead of losing my virginity. She was confused and left in the morning with the money I gave her, choosing to not accompany me for breakfast in the lobby.

Greg: This I don't remember but would neither confirm or deny if I did.

Foot Notes: just a side note here, and I'll preface the side note by saying my dad often says things and when called out later, has either forgotten or simply denies it later on - the side note being my dad has described himself as a self proclaimed push over, usually with the temperament of being happy or else only moderately ticked off but not much fluctuation between these

While I v

*One area*

At one point my dad was explaining he layout of Bangkok to me, explaining sols, I think try were called, numbered sols that was the urban planning for the city I guess we might call it now. I never figured out exactly how to navigate the city according to sols, and for whatever reason didn't really like ye idea of sols and did t want to go near them. I don't know why that is.

*My dads arrangement*

Money most never seemed like something to be understood or worried about or even have any sort of knowledge about for most of my life. But I do remember arriving in Shanghai one trip and my dad asking if I had brought money. I have saved up a couple thousands dollars working at the local hardware store and so my dad said that would be plenty and that's what I used to pay my way interning st the architecture firm in Hong Kong.

*A week off from architecture*

Someone somewhere in Hong Kong told me I have to go to Thailand. So I took a week off from the architecture firm and made the trip. My dad arranged the first day and night, with a car to pick me up from the airport and a stay at the Swiss Lodge, and a friend in Pang who was a student working at the Swiss Lodge, and a plate of fruit on arrival at the hotel, etc etc. but after that I was on my own, and I did t have my bearings so I needed help, and that help came with Pang. Pang took that week off and showed me around and basically took care of me.

*Running out of money*

I never found myself running g out of money yet summer in Hong Kong. I had a good friend in Timothy, who was doing an internship with a company called Little Red Hen, where Denise was Art Director, and so in our down time Tim and I would play the city. I did calculate that the cheapest way to eat was going to be at a little gentrified Thai place that Denise had designed the logo for, so the idea was to go there a lot. That was in Central. But trying to live among expats in Hong Kong in those days wasn't the best way to be frugal and this never seemed to be a problem. I ate coconut buns with a dollop of butter for breakfast and McDonald's in North Point where I lived for dinner. Across the street from the architecture firm there was a local place where we all went and had local cuisine. I would eat a steak with fried egg and soya sauce on rice. Otherwise known as the heart attack inducing choose. Other days we would drive out by the sea and eat fresh seafood. Everyone threw their hundreds into the middle when if came time to pay.

*Rural China Early Days*

*Industrial Revolution*

Rural China the time I was there was not just a barren landscape, but something that basically you couldn't just make up and tell someone about. From throwing live shrimp into a metal casket of boiling water for lunch, to driving by the barf muralled long distance buses on undeveloped roads in the afternoon, in reflection I often wondered if I was in a dream like state. Travelling in the south towards the southern tip, Hainan Island

and Haikou, was our trajectory. But the geographic journey was trumped by the experiential one. On arrival beaches and pool tables embarked on finding a place within the pseudo colonial architecture of the resort e stayed at. I was sick with a local bug, laying in a room in tropical temperatures literally steps from a beach and a pool. Eventually I enjoyed coconuts which were shaken from the trees, and a Diet Coke as well.

*Barf on the bus sides*

Motoring down dusty dirt roads with car and driver alongside industrial era tractor-mashups and buses with overcrowded passengers puking out the window and on its sides was an eye opening experience. It was just bizarre. But for my dad it seemed everyday, and he seemed somewhat happy or amused or happily amused by my reactions. I think I wanted to point it out and say "did you see that" but it was unnecessary. This was his world.

*Shrimps thrown in boiling water*

We had a meal outside on a round steel table, at a restaurant, if you could call it that. The table had a hole in the middle and it was filled with boiling water and they started dumping live shrimp into the boiling water for us to eat. It seemed like a harsh way to go, for the shrimp, and became a story I told often back then. I ate strange things on that trip. After arriving at Hainan Island we ate a Hainanese delicacy or staple I'm not sure, which was simply fried bread dipped in milk. I clicked the moment on my SLR as my dad stuffed his face and it became ironic memory or way of remembering for me.

Greg: Photographs can make it look like you're stuffing your face when you're simply eating normally. Rather unkind to describe it that way.

Foot Notes: to give some context, I shot a photo with my Canon Rebel SLR of my dad eating this fried bread on that trip. He was in fact stuffing his face and often looks that way when he's eating to this day.

*The nice town forgotten*

Somewhere in the middle of nowhere, in China, we went to a town that had one modern resort which I'll never forget. In fact I'm not sure if I imagined it because my dad has no memory of it but it was one of the more luxurious expansive China based resorts I'd been to. The fruit though, was what I remembered. I remembered it as being the best fruit I have ever eaten. That is all. (I talked about it often, much like the Thai rice-based deserts)

Greg: I wonder if it was in Sanya, in Hainan. That would be the place you're talking about just below.

Foot Notes: This was not by the water but somewhere in the middle of mainland China - a small stopover town which, if I remember what I was told correctly, had been described as "a good place" by others who went as well.

*Hainan island*

Jim and Denise and my dad and I sat on the beach at the destination resort in the southern most tip of China, Haikou, where looking out into paradise like waters we watched a military submarine started to surface from below. Jim and my dad told me that backstory of the submarine, why it was there, what was going on politically at that time. I wanted to say what's that but had learnt to bite my lip at that point because expressing astonishment was most likely overkill.

## Heading south

The story here is that we travelled by ground together from Shanghai southward to the southern tip of China, Hainan Island. We went through what was described in an interview as the Industrial Revolution in China, seeing tractors that spurt a bit too much dark grey smog, barf on buses, cars and drivers, food poisoning, everting you could imagine. We erred travelling at a high quality of life but it was still an adjustment from growing up in Vancouver and having never seen or even heard about this type of world before. In fact telling the stories back in Vancouver after completing, I would say my whole Vancouver era circle also didn't know this existed.

## Jim and Denise

Family friends Jim and Denise were a staple in my experiences across in China. Jim was working as a journalist for Dow Jones and had a place with Denise in Tin Hau, Hong Kong, where I stayed one summer. I think I really learnt about temperament of people who were essentially pretty normal by western standards and were just a couple trying to make a life together abroad. When I was alone in the apartment I leafed throgh Jim's CD collection and admired the oscillating fan on sub tropic temperatures of Hing Kong at that time, in the late 90s, early 2000s. I walked down to the MTR station to get around and enjoyed riding the tram around the city and eating fish balls and rice noodles and essentially learning who I am.

Greg: Denise is from Shanghai, so she wasn't really abroad, though she was in a relatively foreign city.

Foot Notes: I met Denise in Hong Kong when I stayed with them at their flat in Tsim Sha Tsui. She is indeed from Shanghai, this is accurate. But she is very globally tempered, and could be a person of any place I believe.

*Pool tables*

Pool tables were clearly a symbol of modern western luxury. Arriving at the resort at Hainan Island, the one thing off was that as you put your head into the ocean breeze you noticed one thing, and outdoor pool table, sitting in the open air lobby. Staff, amenities, cleanliness all seemed normal but then there was this pool table, Jim asked me if I enjoyed playing and we joked that we would grab a game together later. At least in retrospect it appeared to be a joke.

Greg: Actually not really. Pool tables outdoors are pretty low-end Chinese recreation at this point (late 90s). No matter where billiards originated. Seeing the pool table in a high end setting maybe gave you this idea, but as we travelled through Hainan and other parts of south China there would have been pool tables outdoors, maybe under some lights strung up, or outside bars and restaurants along the sidewalk.

Foot Notes: accurate

*Coconuts not too much to ask*

The ocean and the pool weren't connected but were steps from one another. One could submerge themselves in one type of water and then moments later shift to another type of water. Perhaps this was a gimmick but it sounded like storytelling material to me. Coconut trees hung around it all and my dad asked if I wanted some. Staff pulled out a machete and started to chop it open. I swiftly drank what was inside a bit disappointed that there wasn't more and I think I drank cans of coke mostly after that.

*Hong Kong Gentrified*

*bars by the escalator*

Hong Kong is on a hill and during the time of work hard play hard Hong Kong massive gentrification you could walk up the hill and see bar after bar on the up ramp, occasionally stopping for a drink at one before climbing a little higher for a next drink. Hong Kong didn't have laws around drinking age then so I was good to go, and as expats with white skin we had the passport that allowed us entry into this life and these activities. This was bonding time with my dad, over alcohol, learning what it meant to drink and socialize. I was drinking gin and tonics in my formative years, so I was hitting my limit pretty quick. The drinks didn't seem to affect my dad much, he was just enjoying it as I was. Growing up together.

Greg: Hong Kong isn't on a hill. The part where you worked and played more or less is though. Central, Lan Kwai Fong, the mid-levels escalator. Expat Central.

Foot Notes: I spent time in a lot of places. I had befriended a local Shanghai guy named Timothy who lived in Kowloon, across the water from this area my dad described as where I "worked and played more or less". I lived in North Point near the MTR slightly off this main through-fair. I walked up a hill to get to the architecture firm everyday and cabs would often circularly drive around the areas so to keep during that time it was very much hill-immersed.

*Jonathan*

Jonathan Napack passed away suddenly, in a freak situation, in Hong Kong, but that's not how I remember him. I must have first met him in a less popular coffee shop before coffee shops were a thing for me, a quick walk up the hill from Lan Kwai Fong in Central Hong Kong, with my dad. I think he had braces then and struck me as very geeky. My memories of Jonathan and times he was around my dad and I are sporadic. We visited his apartment in Hong Kong, a lit space with Apple everything and a James bondesque mood, transparent sci fi speakers pumping out lighting compositions and dark except for the beeping bopping electronics lighting that showed the space was fully operational. Another time we met Jonathan at a large square footage girly bar, which I have only brief memories of, involving a conversation between Jonathan and my dad, and me as a wallflower being educated in a school of hard knocks way, only the knocks were not hard and there weren't many. If learn by doing is better terminology, let's use that. My dad often recalls a story of receiving news of Jonathan's passing suddenly. It was clearly a major loss to the circle and beyond.

*Cab and alcohol discussion*

My dad has said he recalls I talk I had with him in a cab in Hong

Kong where I revealed to him that I never knew that school played such a big role in social situations. That was the big surprise. It was late 90s early 00s expat life in Hong Kong that I was mingling around so this would be particularly true in the context, but anyway it's not my memory but his. Though thinking back I would say yeah, that happened.

*Petticoat lane*

There were many passages down alleys in Cebttal at that time and one alley off another alley was petticoat lane. I think I just liked saying petticoat lane, it had a certain ring to it, but walking unit mid-day I would be reminded of the sprawled out tables onto the patio and hustle bustle of a Hong Kong evening crowd abs drinks and smoke and life. It was still in the day and do allowed me to let my mind wander on it. We ate tapas there.

*Red bar*

I had an instructor teach me art direction at Emily Carr and it occurred to me to pull out old contact sheets from my time in Hong Kong during this period and show her. She must have liked them and pulled out one photo specifically saying that it was very Greg Girard. It was a photo of artificial light seeping out from a red door, the door to a club/bar called drop in Central. I did t know what she meant at that time. I don't think I knew my dads work at that level yet and just let it pass as a nice compliment. Only later did I understand the impact of artificial light sources on my dad's photography work and what exactly she was seeing in that picture.

*Tapas*

I learnt what tapas bars were in the most pleasant way, through Hong Kong gentrification. In fact the fact that, now reflecting twenty years later, tapas were a trend associated with a certain time period, as hard for me to grasp. I simply hold them in connection with what Hong Kong is, but that is Hong Kong of a very specific time and circumstance, and sometimes I forget that. In any case I remember tapas bar in petticoat lane where we eat and drink abs enjoy our food comas in warm weather, around the chattering of expats and business world social niceties.

Greg: You use the word gentrification a lot. But it doesn't really fit with what you're describing or trying to describe. As a British colony on the China coast, western trends, fashions and ideas always found purchase in Hong Kong. Long before they reached "western" cities in many cases.

Foot notes: gentrification, and a lot of terminology I use, set a stage and perhaps should be perceived less obviously than Wikipedia might say. Also gentrification was used a lot to describe a large part of what was going on in the region then, and the architecture firm I was with did a lot that could only at that time be described as gentrification.

*Photographing the TV*

*penguins hockey*

I was a hockey kid as most are growing up in Vancouver, Canada and had a favorite team in the Pittsburgh Penguins. I couldn't tell you the names of even the most prominent hockey players today but in those days hockey was everything.  So when the penguins made the Stanley cup finals I knew I had to do something.  My dad was in town and my mom and I plotted to get him to shoot photos of the penguins game on TV. We discussed the difficulty of photographing on TV but did it anyway. It wasn't the photos so much as a cherished experience with my dad, the photographer. That's how I see a lot of his photographic journey these days, as being part of that journey rather than the final output.

*Rollerblading by Douglas park*

The first series of photos my dad took of me was of me doing rollerblade crossovers on my residential street by Douglas Park where I grew up in Vancouver.  He had just bought me an ice hockey helmet so I could play competitive roller hockey as I had just made A level and they wanted to support it. I got taken out in my first game, breaking my wrist after a body check from, as the story goes, a guy who ended up in the NHL. I was no longer allowed to let competitive roller hockey after that.

*Slides arrive*

Looking at photo in the little plastic slide viewing contraption was as ordinary as looking at photographs printed out in my household. I removed the plastic foldable pages that held the slides so you could hold them up to the sun and view them.

*Buying a helmet*

There was a hockey equipment store really early on in Vancouver and when my dad was in town we went there to buy gear so I could play roller hockey competitively, but didnt buy pads or new skates or anything, only a helmet. I was happy because it was the exact helmet I wanted, but it also occurred to me that I needed more to play. Money was always tight and I just saw that as our normal unique situation, not better or worse or more or lesss privileged, so this didn't particularly surprise me, even when I was in the dressing room and everyone had a full set of high end gear that they were putting on. I did feel a bit bashful about this situation, particularly when I was in the dressing room, but overall I was a happy kid so it didn't bother me much.

*TAXI*

*kits and dads trip to war zones*

I have one almost cinematic memory of being a can pulling up to a red light with my dad in the back seat with me pulling out contact sheets of his war zone photography. He was very passionate and enthusiastic about what had just happened, as if he had hit a career breakthrough and could see new ideas and ways forward in his minds eye. My mom was in the from seat I think.

*Document China*

*huai hai Lu studio with eMacs*

Really steps from the most notable shopping, be-seen and luxury brands in Shanghai sat an old residential housing where my dad had a stake converting a rental into a studio with his friend and photographer, Fritz. They had a start-up called document China which was basically a Getty images for China. One room had a very large Mac for their first hire to use, an blue coloured iMac, one of the first iMacs which I used for communication with my world back in the west, and a room filled with Mac desktop computers called eMacs, Mac's for education. They ran in the background churning out document China computer tasks and showing off their compute power.

*Phantom Shanghai*

Thinking back to walking in downtown Vancouver with my dad and seeing across the water the neon yellow sulfer stacks that are so emblematic of the Vancouver identity, then later seeing sulfer stacks in a lot of photo work and gallery work made me wonder if I had a pulse on some of this. Phantom Shanghai was part of this as well. Going from knowing the old versus new Shanghai photos as a concept to a realized book of photos from magenta was, or is now in retrospect pretty amazing.

*Yahoo chat*

At document China on huai hai Lu, almost immediately I said I need a computer use after arrival. They had an old iMac in the corner and I was told I could use that, so I could communicate with the west. This was an unusual request for that time but was what I did as an internet savvy person and already could y live without out.

*The hire*

I remember at document China they made one hire from the americas, which sunk a bunch of their budget. They had very large fully loaded iMac for him and a small workstation where he was performing his duties. I did wonder why they didn't hire me for that instead, and never fully came to terms with an understanding around this.

*Keywords*

Document China used a lot of meta data I guess you would call it, and my dad was constantly adding hashtags to his photographs so that they could be found on search, and archived. Archiving was essentially what they were doing so this was a huge energy expenditure. Here was plenty of confidence around using industry connections who would devote themselves to using from and buying from document China, so the priority was to do this archiving properly, or at least it appeared to be.

*Fritz*

Fritz was a mainstay in my dad's world, another photographer with similar ambitions to Greg. He had a desk as large as Greg's at document China and was doing his own work.

*IKEA coach*

There was one spot for visitors, a modern leather ikea couch in a sun room in the space. It wasnt particilarly comfortable do I didn't sit there.

*Apartment studio*

My dad was quick to breakdown suspicions and upon arriving in the space told the story that it was a residential space and they had to discuss special permissions for it to exist as a business space. The Hong kong hardwood floors and general layout of the space were obvious indicators of this.

*Shanghai Life*

*government officials building*

This story was that the gated building my dad lived in, in an apartment that had expansive 180 degree views on Shanghai, was once only occupied by government officials and had only recently opened up to ordinary people who could afford it. A family friend lived in an apartment the same but one floor below, and o often BMXed over from the lane house I was living in several blocks away. Greg encouraged me to bring my bike up to the fourteenth floor or whatever it was so I travelled with BMX in elevator and dumped it in the hall to enter the luxury apartment. I remember my dad had a substantial library, I believe he claimed he bought any halfway interesting book and China and photography that he could find, and one might not imagine that a library occupied or filled with these would be that substantial but it was. Later in life as he moved from place to place he would box up the books and fill half a truck with the boxes, and I would joke with friends about how many boxes of moving that required.

Greg: The building wasn't in any sense luxurious. Interesting you remember it that way. The gate to the driveway was always open so not exactly gated in the sense of keeping anyone out. Foot notes: the building was luxurious in the realm on what you would find in the former French concession in Shanghai during that time. Because this side of Shanghai was often older buildings being torn down, one could easily infer that luxury being described in a building that was reserved only for government officials was actually luxurious.

*Bmxing*

I had been BMXing in Vancouver, not on ramps or antthing, just as a way to get around, and so I tasked myself with finding BMX in Shanghai. There was one shop in the former French concession, and for, after the currency exchange, about 100 CDN dollars I was able to pick one up. It was black and mostly white and rode well enough and despite fixed gear being the bike of choice then I enjoyed my BMX, so much so that I bought a second backup one and began using it to commute to the school I was lecturing at. BMX became a major thread in everywhere I lived abroad. Also to note some of my most memorable times from that period was BMXing around with my iPod and Architecture in Helsinki playing on my iPod learn in g about new neighbourhoods I had never seen before.

*Richmond*

*Richmond art gallery*

My dad upon his return to Vancouver in the 2010s started doing a project documenting a Vancouver Suburb called Richmond. I found myself wandering around Richmond too, eventually find- ing myself on the mall, Richmond centre, early one morning. The mall wasnt technically open yet but I was able to go inside where wandering around the empty passages I eventually found a group of Chinese not citizens doing stretches to music. I had a DSLR with me and shot wide on the group, then shared with my dad, only to find that he had made the same picture.

*The opening*

I arrived at Greg's RAG opening. It was well attended and Greg gave a talk, and in combination they recorded an interview with him explaining his role and personal journey. I b walked briskly through the show recognizing most of the work from one place or another. This has always been a typical reaction for me being in galleries and museums, and to this day is how I view most high art, but particularly my dads when I see it up like this.

*Where is he?*

Where is he was never really a question mark for me. Aside from maybe some really surface conventional ideas about what was normal, I didn't miss having no dad around. I didn't wonder where my dad was.

*single mom*

My mom raised me for the most part while my dad was in Asia for the most part making pictures and focusing on his craft. Having a single Japanese mother trying to acclimatize to Vancouver was not hard, I felt I was surrounded by people and influences that made me happy and made me feel no different than the people around me, aside from being inclined to enjoy artistic of English based ambitions early on. And later on I suppose. But I was not an industry plant in traditional sense. I was just doing what was intuitive for me and didn't know much about my dad or what he was doing with his life in the early days. I don't even think I had a concept that I was supposed to have dad around, there was so much diversity and acceptance of unique situations around me that I thought I was no different.

*Who is this. Meeting.*

I remember meeting my dad for one of the first times. My mom called me away from what I was doing and told me to stand in front of a man. We were facing each other and I wasn't really comprehending what was happening aside from doing what I was told. I was told that this was my dad. I had no reaction of feeling. That was the first time from what I remember.

*Flight to Asia in theory*

Trips to Asia to hang around a photojournalist and be in Hong Kong, a place I thought I'd never even begin to imagine to be, was an obvious yes. I guess I attached the idea that it was my dad's world to all of it, something, a notion, that had never really existed in a digestible way until then. I guess knowing that there was another very different life of someone started to make more sense when attaching it to my dad and what might have happened. People told me he was a famous photographer and that transported me out of my idea of what was imaginable growing up in Vancouver in a very ordinary life in many ways until then.

*His website*

I taught myself to code really early on, after failing a desktop publishing course because I didn't understand how to upload all the work I had done, and then staying inside behind a computer screen all summer listening to all the kids laugh and play in the sun.  This is ordinary these days I suppose but at that time no one did this or at least not on my radar.  But I was seduced by the net, the flashy graphics on Netscape navigator, the tutorials on web monkey etc. and that lead to spending lunch time during highschool sneaking into the computer lab to be on the computer more often.  I dont remember at what point they translated into building a website for me dad and his photography, but I did do that and enjoyed it as a kind of personal project separate from the commercial work I was taking on quite early on, as a teenager even. I remember using Georgia primarily as a font choice, and get minimal aesthetic to let my dad's saturated images pop. I don't remember much beyond that.

*I was early on in the web*

While I was nearing the end of highschool I was hanging out with a lot of college age friends who were mostly studying computer science or engineering. I was playing a competitive card game at that time and they were playing alongside me so they became my friends. One friend, Uri, blessed me with a PC built from parts he sourced that could get me running very well on the internet, something that I had no knowledge of yet. After that I was on the web after school everyday, learning how to build it and basically enjoying a world, a digital world where I fit in. I was PC and my dad was Mac in those days. I don't think my obsession with being online was part of his knowledge base, or at least maybe not until later in life.

*Webmonkey*

There was a tutorials website that showed you how to build the web pretty early on, pre-Wired days, pre-Apple days, and I understood everything they had to offer. When I eventually applied for the design program at Emily Carr, in my admissions interview I included a CD-ROM and pulled up a number of websites I had built. In the resulting notes recommending admission, the note said "presented CD-ROM" and that seems to be why I was accepted into both the communication design and industrial design program, from which I chose communication design.
*Business Cards*

*time magazine*

My dad had a great story about how to deal with no people. People who turned down your ideas or asks for whatever reason hey could make up, these were know people. My dad explained that after he got his name on a business card from TIME magazine and revealed that to no people, a lot of those no's turned to yeses. He told similar stories about having a Canadian passport, and that was something stopped taking for granted having and understood was a great privilege that by luck of the draw I was born into.

*Photojournalism*

I always introduced my dad's early days as him being a photojournalist shooting for Time and Newsweek and Fortune and also doing some work for National Geographic. For what he does today I'll say now he is an art world artist based in Vancouver represented by the Monte Clark gallery. Going into depth beyond this usually resulted in me telling stories about my dad that you're reading here, personal stories, my personal connection. In reflection I don't know if it's factually accurate or not but it's served me well and usually stokes a fire in people, in the audience.

*newsstands*

I often used to tell the story of walking around with my dad in Shanghai, him explaining what he was looking to shoot, shooting it as we walked together, and seeing it on newsstands the next day. My dad explained that it was unlikely that it as the next day that I was seeing these, in any case it was a trip to see the picture that I saw in real on the cover of Asia Week or Business Week or whatever it was. My dad had a go to lab that developed his pictures up the hill from Lan Kwai, and I often just hung out as he did his work there, enjoying the air conditioning and actually getting sick from moving between air con and sweat inducing heat all day long.

*Shanghai overpass*

My dad was already thinking about the contrary of old and new Shanghai In his pictures when we first did photo walks together, but Phantom Shanghai hasn't gone out yet so I only understood it as a concept that my dad was trying to explain to me. Ideas of a single large house surrounded by torn down building, sky scrapers in the background was something that came later. In any case I have memories of my dad finding the ideal overpass to create a shot like this, in our walks together.

*Passports*

I or we often worked with passport visa loopholes. Visa on arrival was an easy one, but another necessary one was that being in China from time to time you needed to stop in Hong Kong and renew your Visa. I can't remember what made Hong Kong exempt or allowed except perhaps because it was SAR (special administrative region) so you could go between the mainland and Hong Kong and stay there as an expat or foreigner. Visa runs they were called. Other places in Southeast Asia offered opportunities for Visa runs as well, but the Hong Kong one was particularly memorable for me. Perhaps because later in life separate from Greg when I was working in the region on my own volition I would take advantage of the privilege of understanding the Visa run.

Greg: Some basic knowledge is required here: Hong Kong was a British colony until 1997. Just under 500 square miles of rock extracted from Qing Dynasty China, in two treaties, in the mid and late 1800s. So, sovereign British territory for 150 years. Mainland Chinese arrived in HK over the years, and for a time freely moved back and forth. The biggest shift happened in the late 40s, during the Chinese civil war, and after Mao's victory in 1949. In the 1950s and 1960s hundreds of thousands of refugees escaping the hardships of life in China under Mao Zedong poured into HK. Stricter border controls were eventually introduced, and China itself essentially banned outward travel of Chinese citizens for decades, but for anyone willing to risk everything HK was alluring and people swam, tunnelled and climbed razor wire to get in. Something that lasted through the 80s and into the 90s.

Greg: After the handover, HK's separate (from the mainland) immigration laws meant that passports issued by developed countries (and many others) don't require visas. So you didn't need a visa to enter HK, because the immigration laws from its time as a British colony remained in effect. Visa-free entry to HK is a pretty fundamental part of a place that has prospered as an international finance centre. But many features that HK used to possess as an open society are gone. Freedom of the press. Freedom of expression. Beijing has introduced strict but vague laws on national security, introducing a level of fear and suspicion into daily life as the authorities encourage people to report on anyone who might be collaborating with foreign powers to threaten the state. HK as you and I knew it is over.

Foot notes: I'll award points as I always have for my dad adding this kind of context to my story. He had been there a long time and spent a lot to accumulate this type of knowledge and I simply parachuted in in my late teens and early 20s. Greg could probably described Vancouver with better historical accuracy than I could as well.

*Airport rebel run in*

I was embarrassed with the camera I carried but it was all I could afford and at 500 dollars for a kid a lot at that. I was trying to learn to shoot with a Rebel G, a Canon SLR film camera, and had it strapped to my body one day when my dad and I were at the airport in place and ran into, as you do, another colleague / photographer / traveller who complimented me on my camera choice and said he had a couple of them on hand as well as backups from his full frame camera. That felt like a compliment and I was glad to know it.

*Enthusiastic guy*

There was an enthusiastic journalist talking about a recent trip to a war zone or some zone, to a group of people informally in a bar. For some reason that time was memorable for me. I remember him moving his arms around, genuine enthusiasm in his debating. But there were a lot of people like him and he seemed to not be a real a-list journalist. I could already smell that on a person, at that age, after being exposed to that world. Greg: Ha!

*Christmas in Shanghai*

I made a splash one trip into Shanghai. My eye lids were on auto close when we arrived in Shanghai at a friends art gallery converted into 20 person Christmas dinner table for festivities at that gallery. Eventually I couldn't keep my eyes open and had to insist on leaving. I think that's when I started to understand how these social circles worked and what privilege I had to feel part of that.

*My copy*

My time walking around Shanghai seeing early images of what would later become the book, Phantom Shanghai, was rewarding. But separate from that it was the magazine work he was doing at that time that was what sparked magic for me in terms of defying and doing the impossible. My dad gifted me a copy of a magazine, I believe it was Asia Week, where he had a great pre-iPhone era photo of a woman in a red jacket on a mobile phone on the cover. His photo. I remember seeing that moment in real life in person walking alongside my dad so this was significant for me.

*Commentary of my dad*

I want to talk a bit about my dad Greg Girard, and present day. Since we are basically in the same city, me in Vancouver and him in a suburb of it, we see each other more often than perhaps we ever have - though almost always one on one, usually for dinner and drinks, when busy, for coffee.

Some of our favorite spots are Milano cafe in gastown, as Greg once lived down the block from there, Faux Bourgious, walking distance somewhat from where I am in Cambie Village, Osterio Autostrada by Queen Elizabeth Park, again in dealing distance for me, 49th Parallel in Kits, close to the printer for him, 49th Parallel on Main, Red Wagon, the restaurant above the Vancouver Art Gallery, or at least under its previous branding, and others.

We talk mostly like any father and son would, sometimes overly argumentative or critical, leaving us disgruntled at the end, sometimes pleasant but still giving echother ideas for rumination over the next week or so. Greg's attitude is when he's angry he isn't even really angry, or not in any way that could possibly sacrifice the relationship, so even if we leave mad we make plans again and do it all over again.

Some interesting conversations have emerged.

Once before he had returned to Canada I met him in town

staying at the Hotel covered in green vines in the west end. The Sylvia. I believe 9/11 had just happened and I met him and his then wife in a hotel room where I discovered newspapers sprawled out covering the event.

Once after I completed of my masters convocation at Simon Fraser University, which my dad attended, we went to Red Wagon in Hastings Sunrise and ate a late breakfast. My dad boasted to the staff of what I had achieved, flashing the parchment and making normal conversation. It was a short meal but marked that time in my life.

Once or twice we met in Kits at a diner on the hill and chatted about death, another time we met there with Roy Arden as well as that was their go-to spot at the time. I had BMXed over and Roy was excited.

None of these encounters were particularly significant or even memorable except in reflection where I, now in my mind, have a kind of scrapbook which of experiences assembled together becomes significant in only a "this is what I did with my life" sort of way.

# 1

# ORIGINAL PREFACE

For now I'll say "Gratitude" (Emerging Scholar: Gratitude of an Award Recipient) was only possible with brave cooperation. I'd like to acknowledge:

Canada's Naomi Klein, David Suzuki, William Gibson, Roy Arden, Don McKellar, Ron Burnett. Humbled to send this group early copies of Gratitude.

Collection at the Vancouver Art Gallery. Humbled to be included here with Gratitude.

Alan, Sandra, Brian, Olivia, Katherine, Yosem, Lilian, Kenny, Danielle, Chick, Meena, Todd, Janhavi, Jeffrey, William, Herbert, Stevie, Meru, Jay, Karla, Enno, Bob, Misty, David, Tara, Vijay, Ian, Jacob, Elsa, William, Danelle, Kris, Cleve, Yvette, Jem, Larry, Kurtis, Claire, Joshua, Rick, Mel, Michelle, Jason, Jim, Wallace, Tobi, Graham, Prakritu, Bei, Mark, Eric, Filip, Paresh, Karin, Paul, Michael, Sean, Cici, Garnett, Charles, Kika, Kenji, Ann, Hien, Hunter, Sam, Sam, Benito, Alfa, Clara, Philip, Mac,

Fedor, Laura, Nagu, Kushan, Sarah, Sam, John, Scott, Miriam, Wilson, Paola, Lillian, Elizabeth, Danielle, Kate, Deanna, Silvia, Ar dot, Predrag, S., Ray, Mrinli, Frank, Wallace, D., Jen, Maria, Tife, Steve, Eric, Migel, Kyle, Kumkum, Tori, Angel, Clarice, Stephanie, Peter, Monica, Amy, Darren, Matt, Tamsyn, Toke, Mo, Shauna, Sheldon, Richard, Tiko, Michael, Lucy, Oscar, Jared, Lisa. Thankful to these people for accepting early copies of Gratitude.

Inform Interiors, Monte Clark Gallery, Kelly and Walsh, Regional Assembly of Text, David Suzuki Foundation, YVR Domestic Terminal, Malala Fund, The Tyee, UnCommonSense Films, Fabrica, Electronic Textual Cultures Laboratory, Arsenal Pulp Press, Great North Artists, Hoefler&Co, Rollout, New Star Books, Lenovo, Equinox, Nielsen Norman Group, IDEA School of Design, Break House Books, Project 88, Emily Carr Students Union, K Plus K Associates, The Economist Group, Full Circle, Culture Days, Granth Bookstore, Art Gallery of Ontario, Granville Island, The Bookshop, Frietag, Albright Knox Gallery, Books and co., Wilson School of Design, Anvil Press, Blue Lotus Gallery, Bookazine. Thankful to these organizations for accepting early copies of Gratitude.

Calgary, Vancouver, Seattle, Toronto, Shanghai, Richmond, Roberts Creek, Vernon, Lexington, Los Angeles, Mumbai, New York, The Netherlands, Mexico, Berlin, Montreal, Chicago, Fremont, Zurich, Burnaby, Calabasas, Galiano Island, Black Creek, Darwin, North Vancouver, Barcelona, Moneola, Richmond, Coquitlam, Australia, London, West Yorkshire, Hong Kong, Kingston, Kowloon, Warsaw, Odisha, White Rock, New Delhi, Italy, Japan, Greenwich, Cochin, Tokyo, Port Coquitlam,

Barcelona, Hillsboro, Mission, Pune, Gurgaon, Seattle, Renton, Buffalo, Surrey, Edinburgh, Darjeeling, Arkansas, San Francisco, Durban, Arkansas, Talum, Champaign, Victoria, Nürnberg, Rajasthan, Philadelphia, Long Island, Bowen Island, Point Roberts, Campbell River, Hamden, London, Venice, Walnut Creek, Santama, Bangladesh, Germany, Washington, Kelowna, Punjab, Denver, Muncie, Abbotsford, Amsterdam, Petaluma, Alberta, Delta, Utah, West Vancouver, Nanaimo, Sao Paulo, Bridgehampton, Beijing, Savannah.  Excited to be in these places around the globe, accepting early copies of Gratitude.

# 2

# GRATITUDE 1: SELECT PRAISE

Thomas is an instructor of mine at Emily Carr University. He has a really clear teaching style and is always there when an extra opinion is needed. I really enjoyed Thomas's class because he is genuinely trying to improve our projects. He is proficient at implementing current trends into his curriculum.

*Rosanna Chiu*

Thomas is an incredible leader, mentor and teacher, who is really invested in his students careers. I saw these qualities first hand, when he was our mentor in a 24 hour hackathon. In the time pressure our team had, Thomas stepped in and steered our team in the right direction. Providing us with strategic and design direction, when our team needed it the most. He fosters a truly collaborative environment in his classroom, and always brings about the newest design trends and practices to the forefront. I am incredibly grateful to have Thomas as a teacher and mentor, in my design career. He is a visionary and a thought leader, who I would highly recommend, for any role.

*Shua Baber*

Thomas' mentorship is unparalleled to any other I've experienced. He has an incredible talent for creating emotional value which is such a huge part of the user journey. Furthermore, I was very impressed with his creative methods of moving through the ideation process. I count myself lucky to have learned so much from Thomas within such a short span of time.

*Jared Zecchel*

Thomas was my instructor for Mobile App Design at Emily Carr University of Art & Design. It was very evident upon first meeting him that being a designer is more than just his job, but away of life. He has a strong commitment to refining his own practice, and this dedication inspires his students to follow his lead. What I appreciate most about Thomas is how much time and space he gives students to take their ideas, and run with them. He provides direction when necessary, but it is usually open to interpretation, which allows students to develop their own unique design process. Skills I have learned from Thomas' class will serve me throughout my entire career, regardless of where it takes me. I would highly recommend him as an instructor, and a design professional.

*Hilary Romans*

My first encounter with Thomas was at Emily Carr University during the Continuing Studies Interaction Design certificate. He taught Mobile App Design during my second semester. Thomas got personally invested in everyone's projects and genuinely wanted everyone to succeed. Thomas has an amazing view on design concepts, patterns and was very clear during all of his lectures and presentations. His class was very hands on and gave me the time to be challenged and experiment with different design concepts, but most of all, truly understand. In the duration of this course, I started developing one of portfolio pieces and it will turn into the perfect project, thanks to Thomas. I am thoroughly enjoying the time I have in Thomas' class. I first encountered Thomas as my instructor for Mobile App Design in the Emily Carr Interaction Design Certificate Program. Thomas is a highly enthusiastic and perceptive instructor. He shares his unparalleled knowledge of design processes with the students in a way that builds our confidence while shaping our understanding. He has a talent for quickly identifying a student's strengths and helping them to advance their ideas based on those core skills. Thanks to his instruction and feedback, I feel ready to take on any challenge the field may throw at me. I strongly endorse Thomas for any creative and educational role.

*Eva Prkachin*

I had the pleasure of having Thomas as my teacher for Mobile Application Design. His teaching methods were inspiring and encouraging. UI research was never my forte, however after taking. his class I learnt to enjoy the process. Thomas gave very useful feedback and really pushes his students out of their comfort zone and forces us to try new things. He's incredibly supportive and you can tell he really cares for each student. Thank you so much Thomas for such an amazing and unique learning experience!

*Caitlin Seward*

I had the pleasure of having Thomas as an instructor during my time in the Interaction Design program at Emily Carr University. Thomas is a wonderful, organized, attentive, and inspiring teacher.  Right from the beginning, he was able to connect with and recognize everyone's strengths and weaknesses, and made sure to help everyone grow in their knowledge and abilities. He was constantly making sure to give each individual student attention and provided positive and helpful feedback, while maintaining a fun and safe classroom environment for everyone to excel.  Thomas is a dedicated and passionate teacher, even arriving early and staying late to answer any questions, ensuring that we were supported throughout our project.  His creativity and experience make him unlike any other teacher, I'm so grateful to have had the chance to learn from him!

*Melanie Deschner*

Thomas provided very useful feedback for me for a major project I worked on.  He is an excellent source for guidance if you need help on anything you work on with his high insight to interaction design. He will be a big plus to any industry he enters with his vast knowledge in designing experience for various audiences. He also has amazing ability to adapt to different environments, as well as catering to different individual needs.

*Kevin Park*

Thomas was my instructor for Mobile Application Design at

Emily Carr University of Art & Design. He catered the course to align with each students abilities and it proved to be incredibly fruitful. In a single course taught by Thomas at Emily Carr, he inspired his students with drive, confidence and curiosity in user experience design. The development of each student reflects his ability as an instructor and mentor and it certainly did not go unnoticed. I appreciate all the feedback and advice Thomas provided and would be excited for the chance to collaborate with him in the future.

*Sarah Tan*

It has been a pleasure to have Thomas as my instructor for the Mobile Application Design course at Emily Carr. He provides a welcoming and supportive environment where everyone can discuss and explore challenges and possibilities. His ways of incorporating new teaching strategies into lessons reflect his passion for design and education. My conversations with Thomas has made an impact on the way I think of creating a valuable user experience.

*Patrick Espiritu*

During my time at Emily Carr, I had the pleasure of having Thomas as one of my instructor's in Interaction Design. He truly cared about the success of his students and continuously provided us with different tools and techniques to carry out our work. He was always available for guidance and support. Thomas encouraged collaboration and innovation, allowing us to take our creativity to a new level. He is a true gem in the industry.

*Alice Vax*

I was lucky to have Thomas as my instructor for Mobile App Design at Emily Carr University of Art & Design.  From day one, Thomas showed such commitment to the success of each and every one of his students. Thomas' innovative and collaborative teaching style created a space where students felt inspired, challenged, encouraged and valued. He was genuinely interested in our developing ideas and designs and was always ready to chat and answer questions or give feedback. It is rare that you come across an instructor like Thomas. The best of the best.

*Sarah Bartley*

I met Thomas while enrolled in the Emily Carr Interaction Design Essentials program where he taught Mobile App Design. His authenticity and professionalism in teaching the class are far beyond the normal way of teaching. Thomas's methods are rich, yet easy to follow, allowing his students to engage and perform at their best. He was able to bring out my personality and creativity by giving me space to explore.  He is always available for feedback and direction when I needed it.  He is dedicated to helping all his students succeed, going above and beyond to mentor us both in and out of the classroom. Thomas is a natural mentor, and I am glad that I have met him.

*Lilian Salloum*

During my time in the interaction design programme at Emily Carr, I had the pleasure of working with Thomas.  He is a driven and organized instructor who develops stimulating relationships with his students. His unique teaching style allows students to explore multiple iterations of their concept, while working in a highly collaborative environment. Thomas uses his extensive experience to introduce many valuable insights into the user experience industry. During class sessions, I have seen Thomas give extra attention to each student, in order to develop their unique strengths. In addition, he is always available before and after class to provide support and guidance. Thomas' innovative and collaborative teaching style has provided great value to my creative experience.

*Ayoob Ullah*

I feel extremely lucky to have had Thomas as an instructor at Emily Carr University. From the get-go he pushes his students to get outside their comfort zone and be the best they can be. You can feel he genuinely cares about his students and their journey to succeed, which was so refreshing and gratifying. I also appreciated his unique teaching methods, like the daily head dumps (which were a constant source of inspiration) and his hands-on approach to learning. He gave us the space to explore our creativity while always being available for feedback and direction when we needed it. Thomas is a natural-born mentor so if you get the chance to have him as an instructor, take it!!

*Jennifer Phan*

Thomas is a unique and creative instructor who truly wants to see his students succeed. His energy is infectious and his professionalism is top-notch. He took the time to learn about us individually as humans and professionals in advance in order to tailor the time in class to the needs of our group. He is a rare and wonderful teacher who creates an environment in which. people feel supported, encouraged, and respected for their own areas of interest and expertise. He definitely does things in a very non-typical way which creates not only a great space to be in but really awesome results. Some of my best ideas and problem-solving processes have come out his class!

*Kristle Bokitch*

Thomas provides his students with one of the best learning environments I have had the pleasure to be a part of. He is genuinely interested in the success and participation of his students in both their educational and professional careers. As my instructor at Emily Carr University for the Mobile App design course, Thomas taught me how to plan a design project from start to finish, as well as proper techniques for creation of new ideas, Specifically overcoming obstacles, Paper Prototyping and User Testing. Thomas was always ready to chat about questions or concerns, or to give me feedback on projects. What I enjoyed the most from his methods of instruction are that he uses his students existing background to direct their work, which allowed us to created informed designs which turned out really well. Thomas was a pleasure to work with, and I look forward to keeping in touch throughout my creative career.

*Max McDonough*

Thomas created an inspiring, safe space for me to be creative and take risks. The class dynamic was really great, Thomas has so much excitement and energy for his students, I felt like it made the whole class so much more excited to learn and to develop our ideas. In Thomas' class I was able to explore the process of a project from start to finish and gain more confidence that my crazy ideas would land, and when they did, how to organise them in a way other people could understand, too! Thomas' teaching style is really focused on trying things and iteration, which is really great because I often get stuck on ideas and wondering if they're good enough. In the classroom, Thomas got us to put our ideas out there so we could quickly get feedback from him and fellow students to see what worked and what could be improved upon. I learned so much about myself in his class and my ideas of my future became more focused. Thank you so much Thomas for being such an inspiring teacher!!

*Christina Loffler*

As a lifelong learner with several university degrees, including a PhD, I have been exposed to many instructors over several decades and it was with great pleasure that I lucked into having Thomas for two courses in design at Emily Carr University of Art and Design. Thomas has a special ability to not only energize a classroom with his idiosyncratic methods of teaching through head-dumps, "blue sky projects", hands-on exercises, and month-long app design projects, but more importantly through his ability to ignite a fire under each student individually. Thomas took time mentoring and guiding each of us; pushing and pulling us and our ideas. He was always at the ready for our questions and to help us through our road blocks, and was genuinely interested in our developing ideas and designs.  I know I'm not alone in saying that Thomas has a real passion for teaching and learning and imparts that energy to his students. Sara Mori-son, psychologist, visual artist, and budding UX designer.

*Sara Morison*

Thomas is absolutely, fully committed to the success of each student in his classes. He challenges his students to use their existing background to inform their work and elevate the value of the group's time in studio, and helps students identify blocks that will limit them as designers.  He encourages students to push themselves past the limits they once thought possible, supports them by reviewing portfolio work and resumes, and makes industry introductions where appropriate.

*Katrina Heschel*

Thomas has been an invaluable mentor to me, he has helped me grow both as a young designer and as a person. I first met Thomas while enrolled in the Emily Carr Interaction Design Essentials program where he taught Mobile Application Design. I am now studying in London at Ravensbourne University as a Product Designer. Thomas is committed to making sure I am constantly improving my work by consistently checking in with me, providing feedback and critique which I have found helpful and quite necessary. Thomas has been supportive, kind and has aided me without any ask for anything in return - I believe this is his most admirable trait; his desire to help all of his students with remarkable care and attention. I hope this speaks to what a great mentor and friend Thomas is, I am very glad to have met him and would recommend him wholeheartedly.

*Hafeez Dawood*

Thomas was my instructor for several courses during my time at Emily Carr. He was an excellent mentor who was able to inspire me to push my creative thinking and abilities. His dedication to helping every student showed and he was always very willing to give up his personal time to offer individual help to every student. Overall, I believe that Thomas is was an integral part to my learning and development throughout the entire program.

*Natalie Lim*

Thomas is committed to helping all of his students achieve their individual goals through his design experience and industry connections. He has a lot to offer his students if they are willing to seek his assistance. As a recent graduate of the University of Waterloo with a bachelors degree in Knowledge Integration (a collaborative interdisciplinary program) with a varied background in work and design experience, Thomas has helped me narrow my focus and better understand potential career paths. He has gone out of his way to help me focus on future directions and helped align the work I am doing in class with career goals. Thomas's classes at Emily Carr leave a lot of room to explore and push boundaries. He is knowledgeable, articulate, and very open-minded when giving critique and feedback making his classroom a very safe space to design in freely. I look forward to designing and learning from Thomas in second term.

*Clarice Chin*

He is a great talented designer, artist, creative problem solver and an ethousiastic instuctor who is always try to share his knowledge with his students with out any deficiency. I found him as a teacher who always dedicated to help and courage his students to grow based on their skills and experiences to be successful. Thomas was not only my unique instructor also one of my good friends.

*Mona Meysami*

Thomas is an amazing instructor who has the unique ability to help students understand abstract ideas in a very simple way. He is extremely creative in his teaching style and is very dedicated to his craft. I had the privilege of being in his classes at Emily Carr University which elevated my skills as a designer. His talent in the industry is translated into the classroom where he pushes the boundaries of art and technology and motivates each student to be at their best. Thomas brings a fresh perspective to every session and goes above and beyond to help his students think in a different way. His depth of knowledge and dedication to design is thoughtful and rewarding. Thomas embodies what every instructor aspires to be, and inspires anyone interested in design to realize what is possible. His mentorship and guidance as an instructor is unmatched.

*Andrea Mah*

I had the pleasure of taking several classes with Thomas during my time in Emily Carr University's interaction design program.

Coming from an Ivy League liberal arts background, I was challenged by Thomas' teaching style to think and create in a way I had never before. Integrating conceptual development with a variety of hands-on techniques, Thomas provided an environment for students to stretch their skills base and build confidence in their creative process. Extending beyond design, his methods are relevant in any field where one needs to communicate and reach a targeted audience effectively. Above all, Thomas is a great mentor who generously supports students in their career development, both during and after the program.

*Misty Liang*

I too was lucky enough to have Thomas as my mobile app design and UX teacher. He taught us current trends and methods of design thinking, prototyping, user testing, and each of their respective importances in modern design. He fostered a great learning environment and he regularly encouraged us as a group to get together and share our successes and frustrations with our post-schooling careers. Not only does he do a great job teaching, but he genuinely cares! 10/10

*Brian Corber*

Thomas is a very thoughtful, genuine and observant individual. His feedback was crucial for me in my professional growth as a designer and how I would take steps beyond Emily Carr into the industry. Our conversations throughout my internship application process to FCV was incredibly helpful as he shared what it was like to be a budding designer and how to follow up with formality but keen interest while keeping in mind about the company's timeline. This made my application process a lot less stressful. I continue to keep in touch with Thomas and there is good reason why. He is a truly keen and passionate individual that believes in the power of Design and Design thinking and mentoring students beyond the classroom.

*Shiao Shiao Chen*

Thomas has a genuine passion for all things design - this enabled him to build an interesting and varied course structure. He excited our class by allowing us to design 'blue sky' ideas, but then grounded us in reality by presenting true-to-life development/client scenarios. He fostered an open culture of sharing with daily 'brain dumps' for students to either absorb or contribute design knowledge. I really felt he gave us the opportunity to shine while provided us useful techniques, tools and insights to bring into the real world. Lastly, his unique and sometimes quirky personality was refreshing among the monotonous lectures and homework of student life. Great experience overall!

*Sam Flores*

Thomas cultivates community and inspires his students to stretch beyond their bounds and push for excellence. He truly cares about each of his students' goals and aspirations. I entered the Emily Carr Interaction Design Essentials program with over ten years experience in communications, marketing and project management. I have always loved design and took the leap to follow my passion. Thomas helped me to realized that having a diversified background is an incredible asset within the field of Interaction Design. In addition, he took time to work with me one-on-one to tailor my portfolio. I spoke with Thomas about my hopes to one day work within the UX team at Lush Fresh Handmade Cosmetics and he kindly connected me with one of his personal friends who worked at the company. I feel very lucky to have the guidance and support of Thomas in achieving my career goals and would like to one day pay it forward in supporting others in achieving their goals.

*Jennie Reckon*

I was lucky enough to have Thomas as my user experience design teacher. He taught us the process of design thinking, real world prototyping, user testing, and their importance. No exaggeration, he's one of the best teachers I've had, and I regularly apply the methodologies he shared with us.

*Craig Huff*

Thomas is smart, perceptive, caring, and deeply committed to helping his students succeed, calling on them to challenge themselves when in school as well as to unreservedly pursue learning beyond it. His positive outlook and sincere belief in community are catching, and have led his students to establish meaningful connections with each other that spread far beyond each graduating class. His approach pushes students to further their thinking, take action on their career aspirations, and undergo remarkable growth as a result. He has a knack for drawing out students' unique strengths and bringing them into dialogue together so that each plays off the others to lift all. Thomas's emphasis on teaching design thinking, process, and methodology helped me build on my own existing educational and professional experiences in ways I couldn't previously have anticipated, and following my studies at Emily Carr, I was accepted into the MA Information Design program at the University of Reading's Department of Typography and Graphic Communication.

*Andrea Wong*

Thomas communicates a deep knowledge and instinct for the iterative design process.  It was a pleasure to study under his tutelage for 6 months.  Learning a vast range of design methods and processes that really helped me in strategizing and reaching my goals.  Thomas is patient, thoughtful, and a enjoyable team leader that really strives for the betterment of the whole and each individual based on an assessment of skills and interests. He has the ability to help you understand a subject from multiple perspectives and use your own mind to produce amazing insights, helping you really construct original and practical approaches to solving really any problem. Thomas was a joy, and made himself available at all times for feedback, or help guide everyone.

*Kyle St-Amour Brennan*

Great teachers become immortal _ they make undeniable impacts on their students, and Thomas is without doubt one of them. He is an incredible person and an amazing teacher, and it was a great privilege for me to be in his Interaction Design classes at Emily Carr. Thomas is a devoted instructor who truly cares about each and every student he comes into contact with. You can often find him in his classroom outside class hours, making himself available to those who need help. When teaching, he is not only extremely knowledgeable and experienced but also has the ability to bring the subject to life through interesting and meaningful activities. That is why the entire class immensely enjoys interacting with him. To me, he is an inspiration and instrumental in developing my skills as a designer.

*Mo Torabi*

It's rare that you come across an instructor such as Thomas. He has tremendous initiative, a desire to continue to learn and a willingness to modify his teaching methods based on his class's needs and personalities. He consistently does this by observing and adapting a no "ego" approach about preferred teaching styles.  I have had the enjoyment of experiencing this first hand at Emily Carr University participating in classes such as Design Fundamentals and Mobile App Design. Thomas displays the qualities that make a teacher successful. He is dependent, motivated and in tune with the needs of his students.  I am very grateful and would like to thank Thomas for his invaluable support and mentorship on my successes as a Web Design Freelancer.

*Jennifer Mills*

Thomas was an exceptional instructor.  He always took his teaching beyond the classroom. He would meet one-on-one with students, encourage them based on their individual skill, challenge them to grow, and help them pursue career opportunities even after our classes with him were complete. Thomas posesses the traits of a great professor of design: someone who is not only thoughtful and critical, but also caring and fun. He is exceptionally knowledgable about all aspects of design and industry trends. I would highly recommend him as a professor of design.

*Kathryn Alcock*

I was extremely lucky to have Thomas as my instructor for Design for Design Fundamentals and Mobile App Design during my Interactive Design Essentials program at Emily Carr. He was not only very knowledgeable but also very dedicated to helping all his students succeed, often going above and beyond to mentor us both in and out of classroom. Not only did Thomas impart to us his knowledge and experience in interaction design, he challenged and encouraged us to apply what we have learnt outside of the classroom setting at events such as hackathons. I am very thankful for Thomas's ongoing support and mentorship throughout and beyond the IDES program.

*Mimi Xia*

It takes years of practice to be a good designer, the effort of becoming a good teacher grows exponentially. I did my design program at Emily Carr University of Art and Design and had the pleasure to meet and study from Thomas. We all know creativity doesn't just come from memorization, great designers have great empathy and can feel the world. Thomas's class has always been the one that bring out our personality and creativity, he didn't just tell us the rules and the principles in design, but rather he used a variety of approaches to inspire us and guide us to explore. I now worked as a UX/UI designer at Conquer Mobile, and what I have learnt from his classes certainly got me very prepared, and more importantly, very excited for entering the industry.

*Desmond Gao*

Thomas has done everything in his power to assist me in reaching my goal of becoming a professional user-experience designer. He's made himself available to meet for coffee, he sends timely emails and he also encouraging me be better on a daily basis. Over the years, he has helped me and many other students to flourish, by teaching us to network and he also has amazing insights which have brought our design projects and resume to a really good place. Under his guidance, I've had the privilege of meeting with talented designers working at Mozilla Firefox, Ayogo and Domain 7. The guy just wants to help his students and the satisfaction of seeing us succeed in life is why he's put in so much of his time.

*Ryan McKaay*

First of all, I really appreciate Thomas taught me something new and useful about design and art stuff in the ECU program about UI/UX + App + web knowledge. Thomas' classes are like good tea or good wine, you may not taste the difference at the very first but the great taste will come out after a second. Honestly, I didn't understand the importance of card sorting and mood board in the first 2 weeks. When the courses in the program had more and more design decisions to make, those new skills were very useful. More than just brainstorming, card sorting helped to choose the better paths for many projects. Basically, the skill reroutes the way I think not only about design but also about my photography work. I miss Thomas' Monday morning class in the Summer.

*Raymond Leung*

3

# GRATITUDE 2: REVISED ABSTRACTS

*Accepted Abstract at the Tenth International Conference on Communication & Media Studies September 11 – 30, 2025 Université Paris 1 Panthéon-Sorbonne Paris, France on UNIQUEWAYS Podcast Report*

The podcast called UNIQUEWAYS is inspired by a series of talk/ workshops I give at conferences and universities and meet-ups. It has had broad appeal. The podcast is more than just design, it shines light on the human side, and specifically on the unique angle that people have in doing what they do. This session considers the podcast and is built around a method called role play, which uses voice and writing to make, test, and iterate an idea.

*Accepted Abstract at the Information, Medium & Society: Twenty-Third International Conference on Publishing Studies June 25 – 26, 2025 University of Hawaii at Hilo Hilo, United States of America on UNIQUEWAYS Podcast Report*

The podcast called UNIQUEWAYS is inspired by a series of talk/ workshops I give at conferences and universities and meet-ups. It has had broad appeal. The podcast is more than just design, it shines light on the human side, and specifically on the unique angle that people have in doing what they do.  This session considers the podcast and is built around a method called role play, which uses voice and writing to make, test, and iterate an idea.

*Accepted Abstract at the Thirty-Second International Conference on Learning July 08 - 10, 2025 University of Granada, School of Education Granada, Spain on UNIQUEWAYS Podcast Report*

The podcast called UNIQUEWAYS is inspired by a series of talk/ workshops I give at conferences and universities and meet-ups. It's had broad appeal touring the international conference circuit, with hundreds of participants at some amazing venues. The podcast is more than just design, it shines light on the human side, and specifically on the unique angle that people have in doing what they do. This session considers the podcast and is built around a method called role play, which uses voice and writing to make, test, and iterate an idea.

*Accepted Abstract at the Thirty-First International Conference on Learning July 10 - 12, 2024 Utrecht University Utrecht, Netherlands on UNIQUEWAYS Podcast Report*

The podcast called UNIQUEWAYS is inspired by a series of talk/ workshops I give at conferences and universities and meet-ups. It has had broad appeal. The podcast is more than just design, it shines light on the human side, and specifically on the unique angle that people have in doing what they do. This session considers the podcast and is built around a method called role play, which uses voice and writing to make, test, and iterate an idea.

*Accepted Abstract at the Twenty-second International Conference on New Directions in the Humanities June 26 - 28, 2024 Sapienza University of Rome, Department of European, American and Inter-cultural Studies Rome, Italy on Unique Ways of Prototyping*

This workshop is built around a method called role play, which uses voice and writing to make, test, and iterate an idea. Participants are first paired up and assigned roles. One person represents a user, and one person represents a product or service that will be interrogated by that user. As a jumping off point, we might say that the product or service is a voice user interface like Siri. Once the roles are assigned to the the pairs, they have a conversation based on their roles; in this case, a conversation between Siri, and a person using Siri. This often happens for a timed interval of ten minutes. After the ten minutes is up, the second half of the workshop begins. In the same pairs, the same conversation happens except this time, we focus on variations of the product or service. The workshop concludes with a takeaway idea. Next time, try this process instead of in pairs, in a group of three, where the third person is a note taker who just listens to the interactive conversation between the pair and turns it into writing. In addition to voice user interfaces, this can easily be adapted to interrogate the relationship between users and mobile devices, or within more pioneering technologies like VR and AR.

*Accepted Abstract at the Nineteenth International Conference on the Arts in Society May 24 - 27, 2024 Hanyang University Seoul, Korea (Republic of) on UNIQUEWAYS Podcast Report*

The podcast called UNIQUEWAYS is inspired by a series of talk/workshops I give at conferences and universities and meet-ups. It has had broad appeal. The podcast is more than just design, it shines light on the human side, and specifically on the unique angle that people have in doing what they do.  This session considers the podcast and is built around a method called role play, which uses voice and writing to make, test, and iterate an idea.

*Accepted Abstract at the Eighteenth International Conference on the Arts in Society July 05 - 07, 2023 Jagiellonian University Kraków, Poland on User Experience and Sophocles*

In design, there is a notion of a maker.  Maybe that person is a ceramics artist, maybe a construction worker, maybe an electrician, maybe a product designer. These people make real physical things that come into the world. Design legend John Maeda talks about the shift away from these craft based makers into a world where people do this through writing, sound, and code, a shift away from the maker. However I don't see this as a shift. I see writing, sound, and code as forms of making as well. Sure, they aren't what we ordinarily see as making, because we are making transient things, abstract things, but they are things and they are coming into the world and they exist within us before existing in the world and this process, this transfer is something I call manifestation of ideas.

*Accepted Abstract at the Twenty-first International Conference on New Directions in the Humanities June 28 – 30, 2023 Sorbonne Université, Faculte des Lettres Paris, France on Advanced Typography Workshops in Quarantine*

The argument is always that design isn't about saving lives. Some people argue for its importance, for example with the historical example of poorly-designed election ballots causing American voters to be confused enough to vote for the wrong party or candidate. Teaching typography during the pandemic puts a new and interesting lens on it. In one sense it is the least of our worries, but historically it has been so important that it must not be allowed to gather dust.

*Accepted Abstract at the Seventeenth International Conference on the Arts in Society July 04 – 06, 2022 San Jorge University Zaragoza, Spain on Advanced Typography Workshops in Quarantine*

The argument is always that design isn't about saving lives. Some people argue for its importance, for example with the historical example of poorly-designed election ballots causing American voters to be confused enough to vote for the wrong party or candidate. Teaching typography during the pandemic puts an interesting lens on it. In one sense it is the least of our worries, but historically it has been so important that it must not be allowed to gather dust.

*Accepted Abstract at the Seventeenth International Conference on Design Principles & Practices March 29 – 31, 2023 Escola Superior de Educação de Lisboa, Campus de Benfica Lisbon, Portugal on User Experience and Sophocles*

In design, there is a notion of a maker. Maybe that person is a ceramics artist, maybe a construction worker, maybe an electrician, maybe a product designer. These people make real physical things that come into the world. Design legend John Maeda talks about the shift away from these craft based makers into a world where people do this through writing, sound, and code, a shift away from the maker. However I don't see this as a shift. I see writing, sound, and code as forms of making as well. Sure, they aren't what we ordinarily see as making, because we are making transient things, abstract things, but they are things and they are coming into the world and they exist within us before existing in the world and this process, this transfer is something I call manifestation of ideas.

*Accepted Abstract at the Twentieth International Conference on New Directions in the Humanities June 20 - 22, 2022 Department of Mediterranean Studies, School of Humanities, University of the Aegean (Rhodes Campus) Rhodes, Greece on User Experience and Sophocles*

In design, there is a notion of a maker. Maybe that person is a ceramics artist, maybe a construction worker, maybe an electrician, maybe a product designer. These people make real physical things that come into the world. Design legend John Maeda talks about the shift away from these craft based makers into a world where people do this through writing, sound, and code, a shift away from the maker. However I don't see this as a shift. I see writing, sound, and code as forms of making as well. Sure, they aren't what we ordinarily see as making, because we are making transient things, abstract things, but they are things and they are coming into the world and they exist within us before existing in the world and this process, this transfer is something I call manifestation of ideas.

*Accepted Abstract at the Thirteenth International Conference on Design Principles & Practices March 01 – 03, 2019 St. Petersburg University Saint Petersburg, Russian Federation on The Helvetica Project*

Based on the idea that designing a logotype without a fundamental knowledge of typography is too ambitious a concept, this project came about. Starting with Helvetica Neue in one weight, either bold, light, or ultra light, we will build a word mark in this session. A work mark might be described as a word typeset in one size and weight of a typeface, with a slight modification to one of the glyphs. One might change the axis of the bowl, or change the length of one of the ascenders or descenders, of create something slightly more illustrative. Ideally the modification made will allow the word to communicate in a new way, visually and perhaps metaphorically. But the important part is that the modification to a glyph is a small change, making the mark only slightly different from the Helvetica typesetting itself. The result will be a word mark which is a modified version of the ubiquitous Helvetica Neue, which can act to build identity for a project, concept, or idea. One might call it a logotype, and they may be correct, however the project is given as something that is achievable within a shorter timeframe and maybe helps a student to begin to appreciate typographic anatomy like bowls, stems, ascenders, and other glyphs.

*Accepted Abstract at the Fourteenth International Conference on the Arts in Society June 19 – 21, 2019 Polytechnic Institute of Lisbon*

*Lisbon, Portugal on One Hundred Watch Faces*

This project is about rapid conceptualization and realization through sketches and reference material.  Considering that we often as designers believe that we must spend time on something and get it right, this exercise is being given.  I've given the same exercise in Shanghai while teaching at a design school there.  The reality is we are in a time when maybe the most important aspect of the creative process is quickly making something to get it in front of someone.  This idea of "the maker" is something that often spurs discussion in interaction design circles, but can be applied to any specialization. Recently "design thinking" has come to the forefront, which might be recognized looking at walls full of post-it notes using processes with complex names like affinity diagramming, card sorting and paper prototyping. In reality the process is cyclical, moving from concept, to making, to testing, over and over as quickly as possible. We work to pull out mistakes which can be critiqued and modified through a next iteration. The simplicity of the project, looking at existing watches and drawing them, one hundred of them, is reductionist. The project is in fact a process of quickly bringing an idea into a manifestation of that idea through sketching, then quickly making another sketch as a result of having made the first sketch.

*Accepted Abstract at the Fifteenth International Conference on The Arts in Society June 24 – 26, 2020 National University of Ireland Galway Galway, Ireland on Unique Ways of Prototyping*

This workshop is built around a method called role play, which uses voice and writing to make, test, and iterate an idea.

Participants are first paired up and assigned roles. One person represents a user, and one person represents a product or service that will be interrogated by that user. As a jumping off point, we might say that the product or service is a voice user interface like Siri. Once the roles are assigned to the the pairs, they have a conversation based on their roles; in this case, a conversation between Siri, and a person using Siri. This often happens for a timed interval of ten minutes. After the ten minutes is up, the second half of the workshop begins. In the same pairs, the same conversation happens except this time, we focus on variations of the product or service. The workshop concludes with a takeaway idea. Next time, try this process instead of in pairs, in a group of three, where the third person is a note taker who just listens to the interactive conversation between the pair and turns it into writing. In addition to voice user interfaces, this can easily be adapted to interrogate the relationship between users and mobile devices, or within more pioneering technologies like VR and AR.

*Accepted Abstract at the Fourteenth International Conference on Design Principles & Practices November 11 – 13, 2020 Pratt Institute, Brooklyn Campus Brooklyn, United States of America on The A4 Workshop*

This session considers a project about rapid conceptualization and realization through sketches and reference material. The conceptualization for this project originated from historical project ideas that were taught at the Bauhaus. In this project, students have one hour and one piece of A4 size paper to make something. The students can make whatever they want and are not given further direction beyond a brief introduction. Some of the hour students have is allocated by the student to decide what a story might be that they could tell around what they have. A timer is set to emphasize the significance of time and the use of time in the project. After the hour is over there is a critique session, where dialogue begins around stories the student have created about what they've made, thinking in terms of a way to introduce themselves and create discussion around design, as a segue into further studies and projects.

*Accepted Abstract at the Fifteenth International Conference on Design Principles & Practices March 02 – 05, 2021 Online Only – Hosted by the University of Monterrey Monterrey, Mexico on Unique Ways of Prototyping*

The process of prototyping is not hard to figure out. Choosing actionable items towards what constitutes "prototyping" is hard. In this workshop, you'll be introduced to some surprising, easy, and effective ways of prototyping which I've taught at Emily Carr University of Art and Design. We will go through different fidelities of prototyping using everything from a roll of masking tape to a blindfold fabric. Then, for the workshop option, you'll have a chance to attempt at prototyping with a partner. We will use a process called role play which requires no knowledge, no creative ability, just a desire to learn and be inspired.

*Accepted Abstract at the Sixteenth International Conference on the Arts in Society June 15 – 18, 2021 Online Only – Hosted by The University of Western Australia, School of Design Perth, Australia on Unique Ways of Making*

I currently run this offering in Oculus VR (social online reality) environment "Altspace". The process of making is not hard to figure out. Choosing actionable items towards what constitutes "making" is hard. In this workshop, you'll be introduced to some surprising, easy, and effective ways of prototyping which I've taught at Emily Carr University of Art and Design. We will go through different fidelities of making using everything from a roll of masking tape to a blindfold fabric. Then, for the workshop option, you'll have a chance to attempt at making with a partner. We will use a process called role play which requires no knowledge, no creative ability, just a desire to learn and be inspired.

*Accepted Abstract at the Nineteenth International Conference on New Directions in the Humanities June 29 - July 02, 2021 Complutense University of Madrid Madrid, Spain on Podiums, Prototypes and Plato: Public Speaking in Terms of Classical Rhetorical Theory*

Plato inspired me to frame and write about my own speaking in terms of classical rhetorical theory. I contextualize my discussion of my design talks within the more positive ideas of Plato's student Aristotle, first touching on his three fundamental laws of logic (ethos, pathos, logos), then I move to Cicero and his five canons (inventio, dispositio, elocutio, memoria, actio). Although these are of less interest to me than coming to terms with Plato's struggle with the morals of rhetoric, they end up being wild areas of exploration and appreciation of the sort of work I am doing in my design workshops and lectures. I organize my narrative according to conventions of rhetorical practice, and in my sub-headings I establish the various sections as elements of a rhetorical discourse. In this way, classical rhetorical theory adds value to what might otherwise be a narrative pastiche.

*Accepted Abstract at the Sixteenth International Conference on Design Principles & Practices January 19 – 21, 2022 Online Only with the University of Newcastle Newcastle, Australia on Advanced Typography Workshops in Quarantine*

The argument is always that design isn't about saving lives. Some people argue for its importance, for example with the historical example of poorly-designed election ballots causing American voters to be confused enough to vote for the wrong party or candidate. Teaching typography during the pandemic puts an interesting lens on it. In one sense it is the least of our worries, but historically it has been so important that it must not be allowed to gather dust.

4

# GRATITUDE 3: LITERARY JOURNAL ESSAYS

*Advanced Typography Workshops in Quarantine: Published text in the Ormsby Review, Graduate Liberal Studies Journal, 2011*

*Saving Lives*

The argument is always that design isn't about saving lives. Some people argue for its importance, for example with the historical example of poorly-designed election ballots causing American voters to be confused enough to vote for the wrong party or candidate. Teaching typography during the pandemic puts an interesting lens on it. In one sense it is the least of our worries, but historically it has been so important that it must not be allowed to gather dust. I teach a class called Advanced Typography at a small private design school in Vancouver and I often reflect on how, throughout history, typography has been carefully documented and considered in practical ways in its relationship with current technologies, in the impact it has on people emotionally and, most importantly, in the way we read.

Letters are meant to be read, and through the careful study of topics like typographic readability and legibility we can assess its continuing importance. Some say we can never see history while it's unfolding, but I simply offer this précis of typographic studies so that perhaps we can reflect, "Wait a minute, writing actually says a lot."

*The Poster*

The poster is the hallmark of typography, the one deliverable that will never disappear. It had its heyday during the Grunge period when cool bands plastered printed posters all over the place, and any designer could make a decent living designing and typesetting these. At some point that shifted and we had to ask ourselves if we had to repurpose posters, thinking of them as a little square Instagram icon on the corner of a screen, or on the side of a Greyhound bus, or in between YouTube videos before the person watching hits the skip button. Or as a motion graphics trailer before a feature film.  The question of the relevance of a poster will of course never be fully valid simply because it has so much good baggage. It's what designers knew and loved and learnt about growing up, and this will continue to be true for as long as knowledge gets passed along. And yes, in a school where we design for screens and try to be vocational to match the needs of industry today, we have to ask ourselves if posters will make the cut into curriculum. I can promise you one thing: those with wisdom will ensure they will.

*Dinner Table Conversation*

As design becomes dinner table conversation I hope that typography makes the cut – so that people can laugh about Comic Sans, or chuckle about Helvetica at a defunct American Apparel clothing store. It's funny to me that American Apparel is now history and no longer current. I suppose that's what happens as time marches forward – your own history continues to be relevant to you and casts a magic spell that makes you smile when you see typographic instructions for a VCR, or the typography of a novel falling apart at the seams in a thrift shop.

My focus on the history of design at this time might seem questionable, but admit that I enjoy talking about the Bauhaus, and the time when sans serifs were emerging, and the time of the chopping off of the serifs, as some designers refer to it during that period; and the illuminated manuscripts that included letters hand-drawn by scribes before the proliferation of the printing press, or the wicked angularity of type during Russian Constructivism. But these are tangential these days. They are in some ways specifically typographic matters.

*London*

I had a trip to London somewhat recently and became overjoyed when I found a Josef Albers original in a small frame around a less-looked-at corner of the Tate Modern. In my course I talk about Albers and Itten for their contributions to colour theory during the Bauhaus. A quick aside: typographic colour is actually a grey colour, which we perceive when we look at a page filled with letters and squint our eyes. Of course, we can open Photoshop and select a letter and pick a red swatch, and the colour will change; and I still feel deflated when asked to convince a group of young designers that colour is not in fact colour as we know it, when they just want to use the Pantone Colour of the Year, or when they have never used anything other than Twitter Blue. Who am I to say? These days the authoritative knowledge of an instructor can be questioned like anything else, and sometimes it makes me wonder what relevance I have other than facilitating critiques and telling stories, the odd one that we can all chuckle at. But I guess that is a legitimate role, and perhaps most academics will agree that the life of an academic has plenty of paradox. Paradoxes? Often I wish I was young enough again to simply be an adult's curiosity.

*Motion Graphics*

When asked to talk about motion graphics I still mention a design production studio that was already history 15 years ago when a professor introduced it to me. Imaginary Forces during its heyday did all the big typographic Hollywood blockbuster trailers, or at least the coolest ones, based out of a little studio in LA. I Googled them to see if they are still around. They are, and they're now doing perhaps the less desirable of those blockbusters, but, I imagine, as profitable as ever. Students have no idea about references that are second nature to me, so I feel sometimes that I transmit information that students will actually read and enjoy and remember, which is a nice feeling. They should read from the reading list (see Works Cited, below), but they complain it's too expensive. I tell them they only need to buy one book, offering A History of Graphic Design, by Alston Purvis and Philip Meggs, for its high-quality reproductions of movie posters and posters for bands. But you can't tell young people anything these days. They might agree or argue, but they will move on to the next thing pretty quickly without much care for what came before it.

*Grids*

Grids can be taught right at the beginning, but that's not how I learned about them. I was taught to experiment first. Only later did I learn that typography had been organized very carefully so that it made sense. Typography really made sense with connected terms like The Swiss Style, The International Typographic Style, and Modernism, and it wasn't hard to prove that even Postmodernism and simple chaos made sense. Still, when I look at a layout with timeless typography, I do feel it's better, but perhaps that's just the bias of an aging designer. Grids are in a handful of things that I teach right at the beginning. Names like Josef Muller Brockmann are connected to those times that witnessed the transitions between Modernism and Postmodernism, making for a rule-based world in contrast to running around like chickens without their heads.

*Negative Space*

One thing I'll say about negative space is that I have typography students who really like to fill up all the space with everything. If they are reading this they should know this is not an original endeavour. The space that's filled or black and the space that's empty or white work in tandem, with some saying the white negative is where the DNA is – it's what we read. I call this filling up of space decorative design simply to make a point, not as a subtle way of insulting something I don't fully understand. And one could fight back claiming that to leave a page blank is no better. What I do know is that elements work together and somehow rub off on each other, in the process tainting our perception of a page. Typography is an art and a science. The practised specialist uses negative space to guide the eye, lead us around shapes that affect our memory and subconscious, and determines how we read, even through the negative.

*Clarity*

So, the next obvious idea would be that typography should be clear and it should be readable. No different than written words, one might claim, as William Zinsser asserts in On Writing Well. Instead of overpowering, typography should recede and weave its magic without intruding or butting in with showy stylization. It should cast and retain its spell after the dust has settled. Type that shouts is in opposition to this, but type that whispers might also draw attention to itself and for that reason could be equally unnecessary. Helvetica, the font, was always the emblem of transparency, but history taints itself, and in current times Helvetica printed and posted on an out-of-service bathroom door, or on a no smoking sign might say a little too much too soon. So even clarity in typography is riddled with complexity as it struggles to free itself. In short, typography needs a day off once in a while too.

*Mathematics*

Mathematics and typography are not distant cousins. Mathematical patterns seen in the proportions of a human body, in the shell of a snail, and in the ripples of the ocean if we stretch a little, are just as much typographic as they are parts of nature.

The Fibonacci series is one example of this: a series of numbers from nature that can work to create harmonious design. In traditional design education, words like beauty, elegance, and timelessness have always been synonymous with good design. We now live in a design world where things have to be tested and evaluated before they can ring true, but believers in human-centred design and more universal aesthetics might still draw on mathematics to communicate, and they would be perfectly correct. Break a page into three equal parts, and you have a "rule of thirds" layout which still stands tall as a soldier marching for math and typography. The curious craftsman who ignores the three sections, well, they are just as susceptible to its genetic order. And when a radical designer makes a jumbled mess, let's just say that it also has its place.

*Contrast*

Contrast in typography is another magic trick. How do you make contrast? Look closely first. Even a blank page is something, and its proportions are something to contrast it with. Add an element to the page, some letters for example, and you might begin to imagine the complexity that even a lazy detective would find, balancing proportions with negative space and an inked surface. And then do less. Doing less is hard work. Two patient competitors both doing less might be the cause of the most vicious battle, doing nothing at all while also doing everything, all at the same time. In other words, even in silence there is white noise, and if a tree falls in the woods there is always a tree falling, and in the blackness of night there is the blackest black. We are always in the elements. This is typographic contrast.

*An Alarming Fact*

If you told me an alarming fact that people spend their whole lives designing fonts, I might think you are telling me a joke I didn't understand. In fact, the design of letters has been going on for a very long time. The first examples in our recorded history are inscriptions on tablets recording ownership of land and other financials, while equally early on are the illuminated manuscripts – labour-intensive and valuable hand-lettered books that, at the time, were equivalent of owning a house today. And when the printing press emerged, people interned carving type out of lead. They might never complete more than one letter a day. Type has existed in all shapes throughout history, and always behind it all were type designers. These days, with a computer, it's faster but not better, even though type designers today are capable and what they create is good. People like Matthew Carter, known for working at Microsoft Typography on faces like Verdana and Georgia, have made letters in virtually all the ways they've ever been made, in contrast to type designers today or in the recent past who might find themselves with a pirated copy of fontlab and some curiosity. In the documentary Helvetica, Matthew Carter argues that it's very difficult to sit on a plane or a train these days and answer when someone asks what you do and you answer type designer. They might reply, "I thought they were all dead."

*Vocabulary*

Kerning, letter-spacing, counters, and ascenders and descenders are all part of this mystery system we call typographic vocabulary. Much like Canadians might learn to speak both

English and French, a designer during their formal education might be forced to learn the language of English along with the language of typography, a highly visual form of the English language that traditionally helped copyrighters communicate with art directors in ad agencies or in editorial design.  The markings on a page using these words is one way that designers communicated with one another through annotation. However, in most Adobe Software we can quickly change some aspects of typography in a vector software like InDesign or a more common program, Adobe Illustrator. But more importantly, through typographic vocabulary, we can talk about those changes and only afterwards make changes that might make or break typography.

*Arms and Legs*

Much like we have arms and legs, typefaces have anatomy. Alexander Lawson's book The Anatomy of a Typeface was evidence of this, solidifying the idea that the anatomy of a typeface was real while finding a place on every typographer's bookshelf, if only to be read by the title on its spine. Much like we have a stomach that can be round and empty sometimes, the lowercase o also has an empty stomach, the negative space inside the letter, a counter. Little feet are called serifs. Type with long arms and legs might be considered to have ascenders and descenders.  Some wording for typographic anatomy is very ordinary, like typography with feet or typography with arms or legs.  A letter might wear a hat, or it might look like a water droplet called a teardrop serif. Other letters that look like binoculars like a g we simply call a binocular g. All of these words describing the anatomy of type slowly cast a magic spell and let us see the world a little differently. Erik Spiekermann in Stop Stealing Sheep and Find Out How Type Works talks about how he enjoys looking at letters while some people enjoy looking at, ahem, nude women or men. Letters are his friends, he says.

*Best Practices*

We need to discuss certain recommendations. Never stretch type, for a type designer may have spent years of their life making the thing, and then to turn it into a deformity in a matter of seconds is horrific. Never use Comic Sans except perhaps for a comic book, since a comic book is what it was designed for. Every font has a purpose. Use it for that. Most of the time the side of a truck isn't meant to look like a comic book, so why would you make it look that way? Comic Sans has a bad reputation beyond this, as something cited to avoid, but I don't see it that way. Instead it's something we should carefully consider and employ for its intended use, which I'll admit is very limited in scope, and which puts it in a corner by itself most of the time. Putting generous amounts of space between capital letters, also known as letter-spacing, is usually good, as capital letters are notoriously hard to read in longer strings of text, and this letter-spacing will help it. On the other hand, tightening the letter- spacing in a font like Helvetica can actually help Helvetica, as we read word shapes; so when there is less space between characters in certain fonts with upper and lower case, reducing the negative space helps us understand it as our eyes travel over the shapes and as we engage in the process of reading. Of course there are exceptions. Spekiermann says you shouldn't put too much space between lowercase letters. People understood it and learnt that, but then they disagreed and did exactly what he said not to do. They rejected an idea once learnt, which is of course is another way.

*Climate*

In our current typographic climate I am often called on to talk about the type of the present day. Which font should I use? Should I pay for a font? How can I learn about type? I wish I could offer shortcuts, but there aren't many. Today type has to work on the small screens of our iPhones, or it has to move around a screen in video, which affects the job of a type designer as well as the job of a typographer. Old type that hasn't been digitized recently often suffers in small-screen environments. Google fonts is an alternative. But is it complete? Type today considers a myriad of modalities that we never could have imagined ten or five years ago. To make it relevant today we have to look at it in these new contexts and ask ourselves if it is still relevant; we have to think about how we can amplify the value of a craft that has been invested in so heavily over time, we must admit it will hold an important place in history. We are the key decision makers for our future.

What do you imagine?

*References*


- Gary Hustwit, Shelby Siegel, and Luke Geissbuhler, Hel-vetica: A Documentary Film (Plexifilm, 2007).
- Thomas King, The Truth About Stories: A Native Narrative (Toronto: House of Anansi Press, 2003).

- Alexander Lawson, The Anatomy of a Typeface (David R. Godine, 1990).
- Alston W. Purvis and Philip B. Meggs, A History of Graphic Design (2006).
- Eric Spiekermann, Stop Stealing Sheep and Find Out How Type Works (Peachpit Press, 2014).
- William Zinsser, On Writing Well: An Informal Guide to Writing Nonfiction (New York: Harper Collins, 1990).

*Dear Thomas King: Published text in the Ormsby Review, Graduate Liberal Studies Journal, 2020*

Dear Thomas King,

Pandemic. I live in a room. In the room there are objects. And by way of you, the objects have stories. We all know objects to have stories. We choose them, buy them, include them in our lives, and continue to include them or discard them. They are a part of us. And the reasons behind them are also a part of us.

These days I think about the stories of innocuous things. Things that you wouldn't think have stories.

At Emily Carr University of Art and Design, in some down time, I had a chance to visit the house of a faculty member who taught a course called "Art Direction." "Art Direction" in this context was about objects and their stories, and the faculty member informed us that everything in her house had a story. She told us the stories as we walked through the house, and in disbelief, we learned that it was true.

Today I'm flanked by objects and their stories. From a Patagonia jacket that makes me think of life in the Bay Area, to a Manzini book that reminds me of pan-con-to-mate in Barcelona, to New Balance sneakers that remind me of my first contract design job, to an Apple mouse that reminds me of dark patterns.

As you note about just about any story, "Take it. You've heard it… it's yours now."[1]

*References*

- [1] From Thomas King, The Truth About Stories: A Native Narrative (Toronto: Anansi, 2003) (CBC Massey Lectures Series)

*Unique Ways of Prototyping: Published text in the Ormsby Review, Graduate Liberal Studies Journal, 2020*

When I talk about "prototyping" here, I'm talking about it in part as I've learnt it in traditional design education, at Emily Carr University of Art + Design, years ago. In that realm we broke down the processes of designing into a number of steps, and prototyping was one of them. Basically, when designers envision and agree on a product to make, they need to make an example first. If it was the design of a shoe, that prototype might be that exact shoe carved and milled out of balsa wood and foam core, not for making lots of, but as a single sample. If it was a website, the prototype might be a picture. Not a working version, not clickable, not accessible through a browser, but instead a sample picture for presentation. It might be seen as a bit of a trick, if you think it's the real thing.

The iconic historical example of this trick is when Steve Jobs presented the Next Computer to a broad audience in a lecture hall in 1988. He actually hadn't readied the Next for distribution, it was simply a single copy that was good enough to use for presentation. In that context everyone thought it was done. Arguably he fooled the audience into thinking they could buy these on the shelves when there was actually only one in existence, the prototype.

*Introduction*

Plato inspired me to frame and write about my own speaking in terms of classical rhetorical theory.[1] I contextualize my discussion of my design talks within the more positive ideas of Plato's student Aristotle, first touching on his three fundamental laws of logic (ethos, pathos, logos),[2] then I move to Cicero and his five canons (inventio, dispositio, elocutio, memoria, actio). Although these are of less interest to me than coming to terms with Plato's struggle with the morals of rhetoric, they end up being wild areas of exploration and appreciation of the sort of work I am doing in my design workshops and lectures. I organize my narrative according to conventions of rhetorical practice, and in my sub-headings I establish the various sections as elements of a rhetorical discourse. In this way, classical rhetorical theory adds value to what might otherwise be a narrative pastiche.

Late in 2019, by invitation I gave a talk at Vancouver tech staple Mobify titled "Unique Ways of Prototyping." Already nervous, after months of anticipation, I buzzed the organizer to take me up the elevators of the Microsoft building on Burrard. No one was there yet, but very soon people here and there started to shuffle about, unfolding scissor chairs and propping up floor banners. One of them danced with questions. "How do you want these chairs set-up?" It was my first prompt. "Can you leave them separated slightly? — I need it that way for the workshop portion," I replied. One of them asked, "Like this?" I nodded.

It was already starting to happen. I placed my bottled water by the podium, a trick of the trade to calm nerves and provide a break in the middle of my talk. This was a talk now. This was something different. I had been a lecturer before. I knew the binaries — the audience's role, the speaker's role — but this was something different.

Let me start with a big reveal. I will say the punch line is that you can teach digital tools and processes with nothing but voice, nothing but a conversation. A conversation is making. A conversation is prototyping. Let me explain by talking about writing, and how writing is, in fact, making. For how ideas flow from your imagination into the real world through writing, as they appear on an inked surface... your ideas are manifesting themselves. In this way, a manifestation of ideas happens. Writing is also prototyping.

A second slide shows three people in conversation. Here, making is happening as well, this time through voice and more complexity. As a person conveys their ideas, the ideas leave the imagination and become part of the world. They become part of the world sonically.  They become part of the world through sound and conversation, and through the conversation the ideas adapt and evolve. This is also prototyping.

And finally, a slide is shown of a round table discussion, where among ten actors, ideas are manifesting through voice, through sound, and through writing, and through a lot of activity. The latter half of the talk concerns how these processes can be used to make digital things. And how at Emily Carr University of Art + Design this is what we do, we make digital things. However, in this entire presentation about prototyping, we never show a computer. We never show an iPhone, an interface, an input/output device. Instead, it's all analog. which is a fancy way of saying that there actually isn't any substance here at all.

*Ethos*

One of Aristotle's modes of persuasion, ethos, appears in a couple of instances during this talk.  I will assume a basic knowledge of ethos and rhetoric, as for the purpose of the paper I am only able to note these instances as I reflect on the talks. Through my Mobify talk I'm quick to mention a couple of facts that don't really tie to the illustration of my journey through "Unique ways of prototyping" at all, and so upon reflection I asked myself why they landed so well, and why I included them. Was it gaudy to include them?

This presentation was somewhat improvised, so I was reading the room in deciding what to say. And two improvised "ethos" things I rely on are my TEDx talk and my Assistant Professor posting in India. As I have come to understand myself better through this writing, I now see these improvisations as Aristotelian persuasive strategies. For example, I mentioned the TEDx talk, even though it is irrelevant to the communication of my personal journey, as well as my linear narrative through the slides. However, when a slide comes up I'm quick to mention, "This is me at my recent TEDx talk." It consistently grabs attention right away. The second, and the point I open the slides with, is my work as an assistant professor in India. It's irrelevant in communicating anything about "Unique ways of prototyping," but it feels right and helps paint a picture of me. You could say that I employ these two experiences try to captivate the audience by building credibility. When people hear these two things, they listen, and they say to themselves "I should listen because he knows something."

*Penn State*

Late in 2018, by invitation, I gave a talk titled "Vulnerability" at Land Grant Institution Pennsylvania State University, at their Stuckeman School in State College, Pennsylvania. Arriving at Stuckeman School after a good night's sleep was very pleasant. This beautifully architected space supports an interior architecture program, which, after taking the tour, I thought was simply amazing. They asked, "Do you have research interests?" I was silent. "We have large budgets for research, like all the land grant institutions here. Here, let me take you for the tour." I was paraded around a beautiful open-plan space surrounded by greenery, in some ways resembling Emily Carr, that provides a space for speaking. "We have a lot of complaints about this space because the speakers' voices echo into the halls, so it makes recording talks difficult. The tech will come meet you and mic you up after you meet a few people this morning."

I had a good feeling about the talk. The work of my past student, Amy, in prototyping using a blindfold fabric was so basic and I thought they would love it. I explained how we could build empathy for visually impaired users with her idea. A person with correct vision puts on the blindfold and sees like a visually impaired user. Her project restored circadian rhythms in visually impaired users by introducing good habits that don't depend on vision.

I kept returning to a focus on people instead of technology, presenting case study after case study about how we were doing amazing things at Emily Carr that take the dependence on technology out of technology related projects. We now design by understanding people's wants and needs. I showed another slide of rough drawings on index cards of what a related mobile application might look like.

Finally, talking about digital, I introduced the Raspberry Pi, a credit card sized computer that is used in teaching and entrepreneurship. I explained the possibilities of prototyping with the thing. And how easy it was to learn. Time wound down and I ended the presentation abruptly as my iPhone timer went off. "Questions?"

*Pathos*

In retrospect, my attempt to employ Aristotle's pathos, a mode of persuasion focused on desire to trust a person, was a mistake. My ideas were overly ambitious for the audience and my abrupt ending made the presentation seem half-baked. I did not address common sense ideas that would help the audience feel they could easily "get it," and it showed. Only two people came up to me afterwards. I had failed at persuasion. Of course, at the time I didn't know it, but later it seemed obvious. The clothing I was wearing, crumpled from my suitcase, didn't help with pathos. My unshaven look didn't help with pathos. And the kicker, the sonically-unfriendly speaking space, hurt pathos. But anyway, my story continues.

*TEDx*

In early 2019, I gave a TEDx talk. The theme was "Greater than you" and the venue was Reliance Theatre at Emily Carr University of Art + Design.

I sat down with Emily Carr University faculty member Scott Mallory, Jr. He was wearing a black ball cap and a black and red lanyard that repeated TEDxECUAD over and over. His brown skin surprised me. "I don't know if you really want to do this." He was already trying to turn me away. He went into a speech. Finally, he asked me what my "idea worth sharing" was, which I hadn't even thought about. "Spending time in airports," I blurted out. "Bwa ha ha ha! I can relate to that," Scott said. He continued, explaining. "You would be a backup. You can come for the rehearsals though." That was February 2019.

And from there I would arrive at Reliance Theatre every Saturday. I perched my iPhone against a wall on video recording mode. I wanted to see myself. Sometimes I would even go during weekdays. The theatre was empty and I would recite to an empty room. "Another dropped," said Scott. "That's four drops. I'll confirm you over the next day or so." The minutes felt like hours as I awaited that confirmation. Nothing came through. I messaged Scott. "Yeah, yeah, you are confirmed. A bunch of people dropped. You'll be the only faculty." A formal email came through. I was speaking at a TED.

"For as long as I can remember, I wanted to travel all around the world," my voice echoed, "but it turns out my favourite places to be are the airports. I realized this was true when I found myself boarding a plane to Seattle just to visit their airport." Scott laughed.

We were in final rehearsals and I decided not to wear shoes. Somehow it felt right without shoes. The talk was about that comfort. About craving things that are familiar. About craving things that feel like home. Scott had changed the order of some phrases around at the last minute in my script. "Another time I was on my way to Barcelona and I was dreaming about Barcelona things." I recalled that trip to Barcelona where I received an emerging scholar award, and tried to make it relatable. "Eating Pan con Tomate, sipping a Tempranillo." The audience laughed. I could feel their warmth.

"It's different now!" said Scott. "But we can work with it." I tried to tune Scott out. Everything went dark. The intonation of my voice changed:

So, next time you are on a plane, think about some of these things. The Diet Coke, tomato juice, Christmas, two-ply toilet paper, seat belts ... even think about Hollywood movies. And think about how these things might remind you of home. Maybe you'll find yourself on a plane too. Just to visit: an airport.

I waved to the audience as I walked off stage.

*Logos*

Viewed through the lens of Aristotle's Logos, it now makes sense how I pushed this talk through. I pushed this talk to be accepted. It probably started when I realized that my talk idea was exactly what Scott wanted. I reasoned at every angle how it was for Scott: how it was about travelling a lot, which Scott did. It was about always being in airports, which Scott often was. It was about helping solve the problem of being short on speakers, which Scott had as well. And my talk was safe. After Scott did the ghost writing of the first paragraph of the talk, I memorized it word for word and recited it that way too. It was exactly what Scott wanted. Scott is a reasonable person and by my reasonable measure, this talk was making it in. The appeal to the audience would also be decided by Scott: the cadence, the segues, the gestures. the timing. Scott's vision was clear and I was going to follow it. This was a talk based on reason.

In Oculus VR [VR = virtual reality] environment "Altspace," I'm asked to host "Unique Ways of Making" every Friday from 4:00 PM to 5:00 PM (PST).

"The future is now." A comment came through in WhatsApp. Microsoft had just acquired Altspace, and there was a lot of excitement around VR. Yunji — that's her avatar name — who works at Microsoft Altspace had walked me through how to run a VR event in Altspace. "If someone opens a portal, just open the host panel and you can kick them. You can ban them here."

I've been putting on my Oculus VR goggles to enter Altspace, checking out the stage, pulling up my slide deck in VR. It's probably one of the biggest venues I've presented in, as the stage feels like it commands attention, the upper level and outdoor balcony provide unique views of the stage, and a nice place to mingle afterwards with the vehicle traffic noise in the background. There is plentiful capacity for a good-sized audience. The catch? None of its real. Or rather, it's all in virtual reality.

Dorothy986 (her handle) and I became friends in Altspace, and she agreed to moderate the event. I muted the audience. With my Oculus headset half on, so I could still press the forward key for the slides from my keyboard, I began speaking. It was mostly the same as a talk I had given before, but I could tell that I was grabbing the audience's attention, which is more or less an impossibility in VR.

"Can I get some heart and clap emojis?" Heart shaped red icons streamed above the avatars' heads in the audience. "Okay once more in a selfie this time! Wait — my eyes were closed. Once more. Okay, awesome! Awesome!" It was awesome. "Writing is making. And talking — conversation is making, you know that now...." Dorothy986 kicked a couple of people "And here we have a group of people in a round table discussion, so complexity, complexity in the making. I'll round out the slide deck with a class I've taught at Emily Carr and then we will go into the workshop." I was excited. New Age stuff! That's what my aunt calls it. I told her it's actually not that new anymore.

Plato would agree. This was his apprehensive rhetoric. My audience was filled with secondary school kids whose classes were cancelled due to the Coronavirus. Others were friends of friends. These were masses waiting to be convinced. Waiting, waiting, and ready to believe what I had to say, as long as I put a little gloss on it. Massaged it a bit. This was not the kind of public speaking I enjoyed, because it didn't require any effort to try to be authentic to land well. To try to reach people; to try to connect. All that structure had already been established. And so my well- intended talk, my well received talk, fell flat in my mind. But in the audience's mind it worked wonderfully. And afterwards my talk would be praised. Like a Plato rhetorician, focused on a talk divorced from content, it convinced anyway despite its VR deception and untruth.

*Unique Ways of Prototyping for Idea Validation*

In February 2020, I gave a talk to Mobify in the Microsoft building in Vancouver to attendees. "Unique Ways of Prototyping for Idea Validation" was something new.

I stood as attendees arrived. Some nice teamwork pulling chairs off the hooks for 83 attendees fell short, and some would be standing or sitting on the couches in the back. This was a big audience for me, but I did not feel the nerves. Organizer Dilan Ustek had brought in her whole network of meet- up.com researchers to watch me speak about research, an area I would love to learn more about. An area I knew little about. But I wasn't nervous, I was this content and this content was me. I knew it well. I lived it and that's how I would present it.

Microsoft had done an amazing job taking a spot in this skyscraper where I would give my talk. Glad to be back; I was ready. Mingling and pizza turned into a rush of people for the seats, but the number was perfect. For a pay-to-attend talk, just the right number showed up. And I was ready: ready to be vulnerable. Ready to be relatable. Ready to be interactive. I pulled up the slides on the MacBook Pro for a last glance, a nice professional photo of myself stared back at me. "Thomas Girard" it said. "That's me. I am Thomas Girard."

"And this..." A long breath followed and I was having trouble speaking. "...is at TEDx after I had given my talk. Three of us are in conversation here." Something was happening with my speech, I could not finish a sentence without taking a breath in between. Fear of public speaking: nothing new. Quirky Thomas Girard. Nothing new. They all know you are quirky. "And that conversation is making."

I landed that vocal full stop and felt my confidence come back. I was in it again. And then my mic died. Almost simpatico a volunteer passed a back-up to me, and then offered to forward the slides on my MacBook Pro keyboard for me. Supporters, so nice to have support. Everything would be smooth from then on.

"So, any Oculus users?" I asked. "Just one? That's so bad!" The audience laughed in tandem. "Okay, for the workshop portion one of you is the Oculus and one of you is the user of Oculus. I'm going to set a timer for ten minutes for you all. Ready?" They burst into conversation with each other. I grabbed my mug of water and took a sip, and just watched and eavesdropped. I made this! I made this happen. I was beaming. I paced around the stage a bit and checked the timer a few times. I looked at the volunteers and they looked back at me wide-eyed, as if they were asking me how I did it. I did it. It was happening.

*Plato*

Plato would have seen this, in his early ideas about the formality of rhetoric, as a good example of his kind of rhetoric. This was my third time at Mobify as a speaker. I started losing track of what was coming out of my mouth; as an orator I was just vocalizing. The rhetoric that has nothing to do with the content. A decorated, embellished blob.

*Suburbs*

In 2019 I gave a "Unique Ways of Making Things" talk-workshop at Richmond's Culture Days, to an audience of 3. My dad, Greg Girard, was one of those in the audience. "You should charge," he professed. "Greg, I think we have different ideologies," I replied. I ended the email thread there. Again, more of the same from my dad. The truth is I was happy to be included in the Minoru Precinct at Richmond Culture Days. I really did feel like it was a big win for me to have that space. It was the start of something. Besides, I just wanted to spread my ideas.

"So, it's 80 dollars to use the projector for the day." "Okay," I replied. Thank goodness my dad wasn't there yet. Three people showed up. Cleveland Stordy was one, a friend who agreed to be a videographer, and another was my dad. The two of them sat in the back of the room chatting. "I'll do a second running of the talk in about 15 minutes," I asked. Can you tell people?" I was competing against a popular workshop next door in the auditorium, the main event there. My dad left after the first presentation and I gave an intimate presentation to a couple who came in and mainly wanted to do the workshop. They thanked me and said how great it was. I was happy. Cleveland stayed to the end. I wanted to repay him. "Beer and pizza?"

A kid and her parent and a couple of seniors sat at the boardroom table. "So, I'm super glad to be here at Richmond Culture Days! There are so many great events going on right now and I feel privileged to be a part of it!" I did feel privilege. But I was talking to an audience of five people. And I was nervous. As I progressed I got into the swing of it. "This is the first time I've run this event as 'Unique Ways of Making Things.' Ordinarily I run it as 'Unique Ways of Prototyping.'" I had only run it a couple of times. I faulted myself for my lack of authenticity. "Questions?" Then conversation filled the room like a warm blanket. These people, sparse as they may be, had been touched. They told others to come and watch and stay. They felt it was something special. And they stayed. They stayed to ask questions. I could run this again. I would run this again.

*Inventio*

I started with a blank browser tab. I started typing in queries. Vancouver. Call for speakers. Nothing came up. This was my inventio phase. To find or discover. The bing of an email notified me of another email. Subject: Richmond Culture Days. Hm, that might work. Here I was coming up with an idea. I thought back to my friend, Stephanie Ostler, a TEDx speaker, who, early in her career, worked the craft fair scene selling women's lingerie, which wasn't that much different. Compose. "I'm interested in running a workshop at your event.... Thanks in advance."

Send.

*Bangalore*

A roundtable discussion in Bangalore, at India's UX [UX = user experience] conference by way of appointment as Assistant Professor at a university near Mumbai, 2018.

We don't have a ticket. Fuck. Get Ashish on the phone. "We've flown in from Ajeenkya DY Patil University." I watched as that very phone call turned our presence from odd suspicion to miraculous welcome. "So, we don't have a lanyard for you — just write your name on here."

It was a packed hotel. I had no idea there were so many designers in Bangalore. I checked my phone again. "We would like to invite you to be part of a round table panel discussion for design heads." My luck was turning. "We would also like to invite you to be part of a round table panel discussion for design educators."

I entered the little room and once again was startled by how nice it was, and how ugly it was outside, the huge division between those who are included in these sorts of things and those who are not.

"Stay." I told my student from Ajeenkya DY Patil University who was chaperoning me, as the professor, around the conference. "No, the invitation was for you..." "Let's get a coffee first then." We approached a server to get a nice strong 4-star hotel Americano, a virtual unknown in India. "Coffee time is over. Hold on." He went to fetch the head server. "Just sit in the lounge it'll just be a moment." Cookies accompanied the coffee.

"Polymath!" The panellists jutted their heads and looked at me. We were mid-way through the round table discussion making sticky notes and I hadn't said a thing. The word polymath would later find its way into the main presentation. "It's a person who has expertise in more than one area. A renaissance man of sorts. It's hugely important." A sticky note went down into the cluster with polymath on it. I proved myself. I was vetted.

The Heads of Departments and tenured professors continued to make sticky notes as if they were doing round table panel discussions like this every day. But I was included now. My sticky note was in. Months later I would look at a photo of the event, my white skin among a sea of brown. I belonged.

*Dispositio*

The structure or skeleton of content for my panel discussion invitation was never a consideration. At least, I don't think so. But there I was, waiting... waiting... as ideas came onto the sticky notes and made their way into clusters. A note taker vetted the best ones. Then, as if on the river at a Texas Hold'em table, I went all-in. "Polymath!" I used to be a card player and realized I had internalized that structure. From that point I would limp in, as you do when you are ahead in poker. Did I win? I looked up at the stage seeing the next slide. Design Heads Roundtable discussion. There it was. The word. Polymath.

*Wearables*

In March 2019, by invitation, I was a speaker in a panel discussion at Vancouver tech company ACL, on "UX [user experience] Design in Wearable Technology."

Greeted by security, up the elevator I went and arrived in an empty space. I looked around for signs of life. None. But this is what I wanted — to feel the space and my presence in it. To know the space, before anyone arrived — before the activity and conversations and Q&A, before the mics and slide decks and banner stands and volunteers — just me and the space. I rummaged through my backpack for my Nike Rogue Ones, the same ones Tim Cook wore when he opened the Apple store in Palo Alto. Eventually organizers started to appear. I put on my Rogues. Luck was on my side now. I sat in the corner as the gears of the event started churning. It had been a while since I'd had such an inviting welcome in Vancouver, and I felt some imposter syndrome as I waited for the other panellists to arrive. "Will there be a photographer?" I asked one of the pink shirts. People started to trickle in, checking in at the makeshift check-in desk. It was a free event and the room would come to fill itself. I hadn't asked about RSVPs. "We're so glad to have you here, Thomas. You're at Emily Carr now, right?" All I could think about was wearables. And how I was going to talk about wearables. I don't remember being particularly nervous, but the nerves always kicked in at events like these. That would never change. I felt like it was my first day of art school again.

"No, no, no, no, no," I blurted out. A knee-jerk reaction. "UX [user experience] should focus on people — why are we emphasizing the technologies?" Blank stare from the moderator. Blank stare from the audience. What was I doing here? Another emotional outburst from Thomas. They continued the panel as if I hadn't said anything. Umph. The discussion floated by and I stared off into the distance. "Are you okay? I'm so sorry!" The moderator approached me afterwards. She was an elementary school teacher by day, completely oblivious to the fact that she was somewhat out of place. "Yeah I'm fine, thank you so much for running this! We were so lucky to have you!"

*Elocutio*

If we denote vocal modulation with a good talk, I was on the ball. "How can you not think about the people?" I wasn't sure if I was screaming at the audience or the other panellists, or the MC. But I was screaming, screaming at someone. I had been mute the entire time and finally kind of erupted. I was glad to be on the panel but I was also aware that I might have been the only person who was qualified to be there, at least in my mind. I went back to being mute. The MC queued me to respond to a question, I looked around the room. There was Eva, a past student. From then on I would talk as if I was talking to her.

*Climate Change*

Panel Discussion on "Climate Action" at Emily Carr University of Art + Design, as part of Boma, a global for-profit speaker series where I would emcee.

"I'm thinking of doing something involving a panel discussion down the line..." During preparations for TEDx, Scott, the organizer, was seeding our conversations. I would later come to know that he was hiding a great deal of information from me, information he would use to weave a beautiful story about his second event that he wanted me to be part of. As he finally explained that second event, I admit that I was seduced. But I wanted to do it. I wanted to see Scott succeed. And I wanted the people around me to succeed. And I would do this by raising the bar, by doing this myself. I didn't mind the extra work. But it was only a couple of weeks before the event and everything was still very ambiguous. I sent a disgruntled email asking Scott if he wanted me to emcee this whole thing, explaining that would be a very different beast. "Yes," he said.

Cartem's donuts had already arrived. The beautifully decorated nourishment separating the massive hall from the hallway. The blinds were closed, and Stephanie was there already. She greeted me and I put on my presentation sneakers, preparing for the photography and videography of the event. "We gather on the unceded Coast Salish territory...." I was on autopilot. I wasn't comprehending what I was saying, the words just flowed from inside my corporeal self and out my lips. I was nervous and there were blips and blobs getting in the way of it being a clean introduction.

I quickly turned it over to the select panellists. They were all eager to promote themselves, telling long-winded stories about what they had been experiencing, not so much about climate action but more business in general. They laid it on thick and the audience sat quiet. The room acquired the ambience of a traditional lecture. This wasn't what Scott wanted but this is how it was unfolded. This was supposed to be an experiment. I looked at him and could see his frustration. He was supposed to give me signals. Five minutes. Two minutes. Cut-off. Wrap-up. I interfered as a conductor might guide an orchestra. I was fumbling a bit but they looked to me to move things along, and so I did. I was emceeing.

*Memoria*

They say that you can't recall it if you never knew it. Sitting down with Scott Mallory at Cartem's Donuts on Main, I sighed a big relief as he pulled up a deck and walked me through what Boma was. It was all new information. "I was thinking you would stand here, and after the first panel you might argue into the student presentations. You might say something like... ." I was walking through Olympic Village saying out loud the words Scott spoke to me, internalizing them. There was some improvisation, but basically I was going to say exactly what I remembered Scott saying to me. At times I would deviate, but I would always return to that memory. The coffee shop. And Scott. That was all I knew and all I could draw from. Until the bing of the email client brought me more ideas from Scott. More to draw from. But I was always nervous. Nervous that a next email would come from Scott which would change my ending. Because I couldn't un-remember his advice, which was less advice and more direction to be implemented.

*Community Centre*

Giving back to 9-14 year olds at Hillcrest Community Centre, Vancouver. "Here's your class list." I wasn't paying attention, my eyes were gliding around the beautiful facade wondering how I ended up here. I was in a daze. I reminded myself that I wasn't getting paid for this. But it didn't matter to me. I was seduced by the architecture of the community centre. I grabbed the list and we walked down the narrow hall, which felt expansive as it overlooked the ice rink, high netting protecting the glass we stood behind from flying pucks.

Eventually we arrived at the room. A worker started pulling out a table. "Let's do a couple of tables and 6 or 7, no let's do 8 chairs," I said. As the chairs were laid out I repositioned them and took out my iPhone to photo document it. I glanced again at the class list, then repositioned the frame of the camera, but again became seduced by the architecture and started cropping in ventilation ducting and exposed beams that lined the ceiling into the photograph. The floor to ceiling windows overlooking the park made their way in as well. I reminded myself that this was a photo of the tables and chairs, and the stack of pink paper, the environment for my workshop. A small girl dressed all in black sat at a table by herself. Her mom explained to me her trouble communicating in English. "Many people are visual learners," I explained before going into my abstract about the workshop. I talked about the use of time, and how when we are bound by time, interesting things happen. I talked about how we need constraints to be creative, and referred back to the idea that all we use is a piece of paper to make something, without any additional tools. No pen, pencil, tape, glue, nothing. Just your hands and that piece of paper. I also talked about how we were to use some of that hour to make a story about what we made. It could be about design or interaction design, and what you might imagine it to be at this point. They looked up at me. "Can we at least get some pens and pencils or something?"

*Actio*

It was a snowy day in Vancouver, and I had only one participant. We called them snow days, when everything in Vancouver shut down. It must have been half way through our session when I asked her how old she was. Ten. How do you talk to a ten year old? I rifled through my vocabulary trying to pick accessible, fun, adventurous words. We would go on an adventure together, a journey without leaving that community centre room, without venturing into the snow. My words would take us there. As I picked the words I decided on the journey. I looked at her smiling and realized she could see the destination.

"What's this?" I led. "It's a fish," she said. She spoke in broken English, but I could tell it was an act. She could have made anything she wanted. But it wasn't just a fish, it was a fish of performance, clad with intricate scales, fins that breathed life into the paper. How did my words get us there?

*References*

- [1] Plato. Gorgias. London: Oxford University Press, 1994.
- [2] Rapp, Christof, "Aristotle's Rhetoric", The Stanford Encyclopedia of Philosophy (Spring 2010 Edition), Edward N. Zalta (ed.), URL = <https://plato.stanford.edu/archives/

spr2010/ entries/ aristotle-rhetoric/>

105

# 5

# GRATITUDE 4: TEDX TRANSCRIPTIONS

*English*

For as long as I can remember, I've wanted to travel all around the world. But it turns out my favorite places to be are the airports. I realized this was true when I found myself boarding a plane to Seattle just to visit their airport. (Laughter) We often think of the world as a vast place with many unknowns and things to learn about culture, but sometimes we forget the things that can be the same wherever they are in the world. Let me illustrate. Recently, I was on a plane to India, and I was dreaming about India things. Greyish orange skies. The subtropical climate. Haggling over rupees with an auto rickshaw driver in Mumbai. But something happened when I arrived in India. I didn't haggle over rupees. I took a taxi. Another time, I was on my way to Barcelona, and I was dreaming about Barcelona things. Immersed in Gaudi architecture. Eating pan con tomate. Sipping a tempranillo. Something happened there too. I didn't sip a tempranillo. I ordered a Diet Coke. (Laughter) And a second Diet Coke to save for later. Something happens when we're in unfamiliar situations like these. We seek things that are familiar. We actually crave things that are familiar. Next time you're on a plane, think about some of these things. Think about the Diet Coke. The tomato juice. Christmas. Two-ply toilet paper. Seat belts. Even think about Hollywood movies. And think about how these things might remind you of home. Maybe you'll find yourself on a plane too. Just to visit an airport. Thank you. (Applause)

*Spanish*

Desde que tengo memoria, he querido viajar alrededor del mundo. Sin embargo, resulta que mis lugares favoritos son los aeropuertos. Me di cuenta de esto cuando me vi abordando un avión a Seattle solo para visitar su aeropuerto. (Risas) Siempre pensamos que el mundo es un enorme lugar con muchas incognitas y cosas culturales que aprender, pero a veces olvidamos las cosas que pueden ser iguales en cualquier parte del mundo. Déjenme mostrarles. Hace poco, estaba en un avión a la India y estaba soñando sobre cosas de la India. Cielos de color naranja grisáceo. El clima subtropical. Regateando rupias con un conductor de autorickshaw en Mumbai. Sin embargo, algo pasó cuando llegué a la India. No regateé rupias. Tomé un taxi. En otra ocasión, estaba volando a Barcelona y soñaba sobre cosas de Barcelona. Inmerso en la arquitectura de Gaudí. Comiendo pan con tomate. Bebiendo un tempranillo. Algo pasó allí también. No bebí un tempranillo. Pedí una Coca Light. (Risas) Y una segunda Coca Light para más tarde. Algo pasa cuando estamos en situaciones desconocidas como estas. Buscamos cosas que son familiares. De hecho anhelamos cosas que son familiares. La próxima vez que estés en un avión, piensen en alguna de estas cosas. Piensen en la Coca Light. En el jugo de tomate. Navidad. Papel higiénico de dos capas. Cinturones de seguridad. Incluso piensen en las películas de Hollywood. Y piensen en cómo estas cosas podrían recordarles su propio hogar. Quizás también se vean en un vuelo, simplemente para visitar un aeropuerto. Gracias. (Aplausos)

*French*

D'aussi loin que je me souvienne, j'ai toujours voulu voyager partout dans le monde. Mais en fait, mes endroits préférés sont les aéroports. J'en ai pris conscience lorsque je me suis retrouvé à prendre l'avion pour Seattle, juste pour visiter l'aéroport. (rires) Pour nous, le monde est un vaste endroit rempli d'inconnus et de choses à apprendre sur la culture. Mais parfois, on oublie ces choses qui peuvent être les mêmes où qu'elles soient dans le monde. Je m'explique. Récemment, j'ai pris l'avion pour l'Inde, et je rêvais en pensant à toutes ces images que l'on associe à l'Inde. Le ciel orange tirant sur le gris. Le climat subtropical. Négocier avec le conducteur de pousse- pousse à Mumbai. Mais une fois arrivé en Inde, il s'est passé quelque chose. Je n'ai pas négocié. J'ai pris un taxi. Une autre fois, je me rendais à Barcelone, et je rêvais en pensant à toutes ces images que l'on associe à Barcelone. Me plonger dans l'architecture de Gaudí. Manger du pan con tomate. Siroter un tempranillo. Il s'est passé quelque chose aussi là-bas. Je n'ai pas siroté de tempranillo. J'ai commandé un Coca-Cola Light. (rires) Et un deuxième pour plustard. Il se passe quelque chose quand on fait face à des situations peu familières. Nous cherchons des choses familières. En fait, on meurt d'envie de retrouver des choses familières. Quand vous prendrez l'avion, pensez à ces choses. Pensez au Coca-Cola Light. Au jus de tomate. A Noël. Au papier toilette double épaisseur. Aux ceintures de sécurité. Pensez même aux films hollywoodiens. Et voyez comment ces choses peuvent vous être familières. Vous vous retrouverez peut-être aussi dans un avion, simplement pour visiter un aéroport. Merci. (applaudissements)

*Italian*

Fin da quando ho memoria ho sempre voluto viaggiare per il mondo. Ma ho scoperto che i miei posti preferiti sono gli aeroporti. L'ho realizzato quando mi sono ritrovato su di un volo per Seattle solamente per visitare l'aeroporto. (Risate) Pensiamo spesso al mondo come un luogo vasto con molte incognite e nuove cose da imparare riguardo la cultura, ma a volte dimentichiamo le cose che possono essere le stesse in qualunque parte del mondo. Lasciatemi spiegare. Recentemente ero su un aereo per l'India e stavo sognando delle cose indiane. Cieli di un arancio grigiastro, clima subtropicale, contrattare per delle rupie con un pilota di risciò a motore a Mumbai. Ma è successo qualcosa quando sono arrivato in India. Non ho contrattato per le rupie, ho preso un taxi. Un'altra volta, ero in viaggio per Barcellona e stavo sognando le cose di Barcellona. Immersa nell'architettura di Gaudì, mangiando pan con tomate, sorseggiando Tempranillo. Ma è successo qualcosa anche lì. Non ho bevuto Tempranillo, ho ordinato una Diet Coke. (Risate) E un'altra Diet Coke per dopo. Succede qualcosa quando ci si trova in situazioni così insolite. Si cerca ciò che è familiare, veramente si brama ciò che è familiare. La prossima volta che siete su un aereo, pensate ad alcune di queste cose. Pensate alla Diet Coke, la salsa di pomodoro, il Natale, la carta igienica doppio strato, cinture di sicurezza, pensate persino ai film di Hollywood. Pensate a come queste cose potrebbero ricordarvi casa. Magari vi troverete anche voi su un aereo, solamente per visitare un aeroporto. Grazie. (Applausi)

*Norwegian*

Så lenge jeg kan huske, har jeg ønsket å reise verden rundt. Men det viser seg at favorittstedene mine er flyplassene. Jeg skjønte at dette var sant da jeg fant meg selv ombord på et fly til Seattle bare for å besøke flyplassen deres. (Latter) Vi tenker ofte på verden som et stort sted med mange ukjente og ting å lære om kultur, men noen ganger glemmer vi tingene som kan være de samme uansett hvor de er i verden. La meg illustrere. Nylig var jeg på et fly til India, og jeg drømte om India-ting. Gråaktig oransje himmel. Det subtropiske klimaet. Prute over rupier med en rickshaw-sjåfør i Mumbai. Men noe skjedde da jeg ankom India. Jeg prutet ikke over rupier. Jeg tok taxi. En annen gang, var jeg på vei til Barcelona, og jeg drømte om ting fra Barcelona. Fordypet i Gaudi-arkitektur. Spise pan con tomate. Nipper til en tempranillo. Noe skjedde der også. Jeg nippet ikke til en tempranillo. Jeg bestilte en Diet Coke. (Latter) Og en annen Diet Coke for senere. Noe skjer når vi er i ukjente situasjoner som disse. Vi søker ting som er kjent. Vi lengter faktisk etter ting som er kjent. Neste gang du er på et fly, tenk på noen av disse tingene. Tenk på Diet Coke. Tomatsaften. Jul. To-lags toalettpapir. Setebelter. Tenk på Hollywood-filmer. Og tenk på hvordan disse tingene kan minne deg om hjem. Kanskje du finner deg selv i et fly. Bare for å besøke en flyplass. Takk skal du ha. (Applaus)

*Portuguese Brazilian*

Desde que me lembro, eu queria viajar ao redor do mundo. Mas acontece que meus lugares favoritos são os aeroportos. Percebi que isso era verdade quando me encontrei embarcando num avião pra Seattle, apenas para visitar o aeroporto de lá. (Risos) Muitas vezes pensamos no mundo como um vasto lugar a ser explorado e cheio de coisas a se aprender sobre cultura, mas às vezes nos esquecemos das coisas que podem ser o mesmo onde quer que estejam no mundo. Deixe-me ilustrar. Recentemente, eu estava em um avião para a Índia, e eu estava sonhando sobre as coisas da Índia. Céus laranja acinzentados. O clima subtropical. Pechinchar rúpias com um motorista de auto-riquixá em Mumbai. Mas algo aconteceu quando cheguei à Índia. Eu não pechincheirúpias. Eu peguei um táxi. Numa outra vez, eu estava a caminho de Barcelona, e eu estava sonhando com as coisas de Barcelona. Imergir na arquitetura de Gaudi. Comer pão com tomate. Beber um tempranillo. Algo aconteceu lá também. Não bebi um tempranillo. Pedi uma Coca diet. (Risos) E uma segunda Coca diet para mais tarde. Algo acontece quando estamos em situações desconhecidas como estas. Procuramos coisas que são familiares. Realmente ansiamos por coisas que são familiares. Da próxima vez que estiver num avião, pense em algumas dessas coisas. Pense na Coca diet. No suco de tomate. Natal. Papel higiênico de folha dupla. Cintos de segurança. Pense até em filmes de Hollywood. E pense em como essas coisas podem te lembrar de casa. Talvez você se encontre em um avião também. Apenas para visitar um aeroporto. Obrigado.

(Aplausos)

*Portuguese*

Desde que me lembro que queria viajar à volta do mundo. Mas acontece que os meus locais preferido são os aeroportos. Percebi que isto era assim quando me encontrei num avião para Seattle apenas para visitar o aeroporto. (Risos) Muitas vezes pensamos no mundo como um vasto local de coisas desconhecidas e coisas a aprender sobre culturas, mas, por vezes, esquecemos que as coisas podem ser as mesmas onde quer que se encontrem no mundo, Vou ilustrar o que digo. Há pouco tempo, eu ia num avião para a Índia e estava a sonhar com as coisas da Índia. Céus laranja acinzentados, um clima subtropical. Regatear rupias com um condutor de riquexó em Mumbai. Mas aconteceu uma coisa quando cheguei à Índia. Não regateeirupias. Apanhei um táxi. De outra vez, estava a caminho de Barcelona, e sonhava com as coisas em Barcelona. Mergulhado na arquitetura de Gaudi. A comer pão com tomate. A beberricar um "tempranillo". Também ali aconteceu uma coisa. Não beberriquei um "tempranillo". Pedi uma Diet Coke. (Risos) E uma segunda Diet Coke, para daí a bocado. Acontece qualquer coisa quando estamos em situações desconhecidas como estas. Procuramos coisas que conhecemos. Desejamos coisas que são conhecidas. Da próxima vez que estiverem num avião, pensem nalgumas destas coisas. Pensem na Diet Coke. No sumo de tomate. No Natal. No papel higiénico de duas folhas. Nos cintos de segurança. Pensem até nos filmes de Hollywood. Pensem em como essas coisas nos fazem lembrar a nossa terra. Talvez também se encontrem num avião apenas para visitar um aeroporto. Obrigado. (Aplausos)

*Swedish*

Så länge jag kan minnas, jag har velat resa runt om i världen. Men det visar sig att mina favoritplatser är flygplatserna. Jag insåg att detta var sant när jag gick ombord på ett flygplan till Seattle bara för att besöka deras flygplats. (Skratt) Vi tänker ofta på världen som en storplats med många okända faktorer och saker att lära sig om kultur, men ibland glömmer vi sakerna det kan vara detsamma var de än är i världen. Låt mig illustrera. Nyligen var jag på ett plan till Indien och jag drömde om indiska saker. Grå-orangea himlar. Det subtropiskaklimatet. Pruta över rupier med en motor-rickshawförare i Mumbai. Men något hände när jag kom till Indien. Jag prutade inte över rupier. Jag tog en taxi. En annan gång var jag på väg till Barcelona och jag drömde om Barcelonasaker. Nedsänkt i Gaudi-arkitektur. Äta spanskt tomatbröd. Smuttar på en tempranillo. Något hände också där. Jag smuttade inte på någon tempranillo. Jag beställde en Diet Coke. (Skratt) Och en andra Diet Coke för att spara till senare. Något händer när vi är i okända situationer som dessa. Vi söker saker som är bekanta. Vi önskar faktiskt saker som är bekanta. Nästa gång du är på ett plan tänk på några av dessa saker. Tänk på Diet Coke. Tomatsaft. Jul. Dubbelt toalettpapper. Säkerhetsbälten. Tänk även på Hollywood-filmer. Och tänk på hur dessa saker kanske påminner dig om hemmet. Kanske märker du också att du sitter på ett plan. Bara för att besöka en flygplats. Tack. (Applåder)

*Turkish*

Kendimi bildim bileli dünyayı dolaşmak istiyorum. Anlaşıldı ki en sevdiğimyerler havaalanları. Kendimi yalnızca havaalanını görmek için Seattle'a uçak bileti ararken bulduğumda bunu fark ettim. (Kahkaha) Genelde dünyayı birçok bilinmeyeni ve öğrenilecek kültürel birçok şeyi olan bir yer olarak düşünüyoruz. ancak bazen dünyanın her yerinde aynı olan şeyleri unutuyoruz. Açıklayayım. Geçtiğimiz günlerde Hindistan'a giden bir uçaktaydım ve Hindistan'a özgü şeyleri düşünüyordum. Griye çalan turuncu gökyüzü. Subtropikaliklim. Mumbai'de bir üç tekerlekli sürücüsüyle pazarlığa tutuşmak. Ama Hindistan'a vardığımda bir şeyler oldu. Üç tekerlekliler için pazarlığa tutuşmadım. Bir taksi tuttum. Başka bir zaman da Barselona yolundayken Barselona'ya özgü şeyleri düşünüyordum. Gauidi mimarisine dalıp gitmiştim. Pan con tomate yemek. Tempranillo içmek. Orada da bir şeyler oldu. Tempranillo içemedim. Diyet kola sipariş ettim. (Kahkaha) Daha sonra içmek için bir tane daha söyledim. Böyle alışılmadık durumlarda hep bir şeyler olur zaten. Alıştığımız bir şeylerin peşine düşeriz. Alıştığımız şeyleri çeker canımız. Bir daha ki sefere bir uçağa bindiğinizde bunları bir düşünün. Diyet kolayı bir düşünün. Domates suyunu. Noeli. İki katlı tuvalet kağıdını. Emniyet kemerlerini. Hatta Hollywood filmlerini. Böyle şeylerin size nasıl evi hatırlattığını bir düşünün. Belki bir gün siz de kendinizi bir uçakta bulursunuz, sırf bir havaalanını görmek için bindiğiniz bir uçakta. Teşekkürler. (Alkış)


*Greek*


Από τότε που θυμάμαι τον εαυτό μου, ηθελα να ταξιδέψω σε ολον τον κόσμο. Αλλά τελικά τα αγαπημένα μου μέρη είναι τα αεροδρόμια. Το συνειδητοποίησα όταν βρέθηκα να επιβιβάζομαι σε ένα αεροπλάνο για το Σιάτλ μόνο και μόνο για να επισκεφτώ το αεροδρόμιότους. (Γελια)

Συχνά σκεφτόμαστε τον κόσμο ως ένα αχανές μέρος με πολλά άγνωστα και πράγματα που αξίζει να μάθουμε για τους πολιτισμούς, αλλά μερικές φορές ξεχνάμε αυτά που μπορεί να είναι τα ίδια όπου και να βρίσκονται στον κόσμο. Θα σας δώσω ένα παράδειγμα. Πρόσφατα, πέταγα για Ινδία, και ονειρευόμουν πράγματα σχετικά με την Ινδία. Γκριζοπορτοκαλί ουρανούς. Το υποτροπικό κλίμα. Να κάνω παζάρια σε ρουπίες με έναν οδηγό τρίκυκλου στη Μουμπάι. Αλλά κάτι συνέβη όταν έφτασα στην Ινδία. Δεν έκανα παζάρια σε ρουπίες. Πήρα ένα ταξί. Μια άλλη φορά, πήγαινα στη Βαρκελόνη, και ονειρευόμουν πράγματα σχετικά με την Βαρκελόνη. Να βυθίζομαι στην αρχιτεκτονική του Γκαουντί. Να τρώω ψωμί με ντομάτα. Να πίνω κρασί Τεμπρανίγιο. Αλλά κάτι συνέβη κι εκεί. Δεν ήπια Τεμπρανίγιο. Παράγγειλα Coca Cola Light. (Γέλια) Και μια δεύτερη Coca Cola Light για μετά. Κάτι συμβαίνει όταν βρισκόμαστε σε άγνωστες καταστάσεις όπως αυτή. Αναζητούμε αυτά που μας είναι γνώριμα. Στην πραγματικότητα, λαχταρούμε αυτά που μας είναι γνώριμα. Την επόμενη φορά που θα είστε σε ένα αεροπλάνο, σκεφτείτε μερικά από αυτά. Σκεφτείτε την Coca Cola Light. Τον τοματοχυμό. Τα Χριστούγεννα. Το διπλό χαρτί υγείας. Τις ζώνες ασφαλείας. Σκεφτείτε μέχρι και τις Χολιγουντιανές ταινίες. Και σκεφτείτε πώς αυτά τα πράγματα σας θυμίζουν το σπίτι σας. Ίσως να βρεθείτε κι εσείς πάνω σε ένα αεροπλάνο. Απλώς για να επισκεφτείτε ένα αεροδρόμιο. Σας ευχαριστώ. (Χειροκρότημα)

*Russian*

Сколько я себя помню, я всегда хотел путешествовать

по миру. Но оказывается, мои любимые места — аэропорты. Я понял это, когда садился в самолёт в Сиэтле, — просто чтобы побыть в аэропорту. (Смех) Мы часто представляем мир огромным, неизведанным, с культурными различиями, но иногда забываем о вещах, которыепохожи, где бы они ни находились. Приведу наглядный пример. Недавно я летел вИндию и мечтал о том, что я там увижу. Серовато-оранжевое небо. Субтропический климат. Спор из-за стоимости поездки с водителем рикши в Мумбае. Но что-то произошло, когда я приехал в Индию. Я не спорил по поводу цены поездки. Я взял такси. В другой раз, по пути в Барселону, я представлял себя в Барселоне погружённым в архитектуру Гауди, жующим хлеб с помидорами и потягивающим темпранильо. Но и там кое-что произошло. Я не пил темпранильо. Я заказал диетическую колу. (Смех) И вторую, такую же, я оставил на потом. Что-то происходит, когда мы в незнакомых ситуациях, подобных этим. Мы ищем привычные нам вещи. На самом деле мы мечтаем о знакомых нам вещах. В следующий раз, находясь на борту самолёта, подумайте о них. Подумайте о диетической коле, о томатном соке, Рождестве, двухслойной туалетной бумаге, о ремнях безопасности и даже о голливудских фильмах. И подумайте, как эти вещи могут напоминать вам о доме. Может, и вы тоже окажетесь в самолёте, только чтобы побывать в аэропорту. Спасибо. (Аплодисменты)

*Kurdish*

هەتا بیرم بێت و سیستەمەوە گەشتە بە هەموو جیهاندا بکەم. بەماڵەی ئەوە دەرکەوت کە شوێنی خۆشکانەکەم بوی بۆ بچم بۆ کۆرفەخانەکان. زانیم ئەمەی پراستە کاتێک خۆم دەیتەوە دانیشتووم لە وان کۆرفەکەیە بۆ سیاتل تەنها بۆ سەردانی

کۆرفەخانەکە (پێکیە نینە) ئەمەی رۆژ بیر لە جیهان دەکەم. چەندین لەگەڵ هەروەگ ی شوێنیکەی وەهوونیەکەد نەنەسراو کۆرفەخانە هەندێک بەماڵ، کلتوری بەرابەری فریبوون بۆ شتەکانا و راج شتەکان لەل بەریدەکە نین کە دەکریت هەمان تش بیت سەردانی بۆ بوومە هیندستان، و من. لەم داواینادە، لە کۆرفەکەیە بووم بۆ هیندستان، و من. هەرکەس ی کۆ کەیەی جیهانەکە بن. ئابن. من پرووینبیکەمەوە. ئیسمانی خونوم دەبینی دەربارەی شتەکانی هیندستان. کە شە و هەواای نمیمچ هە خولگ ی هیی. پرتەقاڵی خۆڵەمێشی. بازرگانی بە پارەی ووپی لەگەڵ شۆفێری دەست گرتێ لە مۆمبای. بەماڵ شتێک کا ڕوویدا کاتێک گەیشتمە هیندستان. من سوەدا بە پارەی ووپی نەکردە. منات کا سیی هەکم گرت. جارێکی تر، من لە ڕێگە بووم ۆن نە، و خونوم بە شتەکانی بەرشە لۆنە دەوە. چووم وان تەرال سازیی گۆدی. نان و تەماتە خواردر. قومیێک ی لە شەراپاب ی دا. لۆیێ شتێکی تر قووم. من تیێم پرە نەڵۆدنە دا. من واد ای خواردنە هوودوو خواردنەوەیکۆی داتیکرد. (پێکی نینە) کۆی داتی بۆی هەوەی داوتر ب پاریێزیت. شتێک رۆدو دە دات ک ئاتێک ی ئەمەی لە حاڵەتە نابا وان کلەم جۆرەینئ. ئەودەوای ئەو شتانادە هەرەگ ئی نن کە باون. جارێ داهاوتو کە لەکۆرف ەخواردنەوەی کۆڵەکی لەم شتاتنە بە ریب لە هەندێک کۆڵەکی یخواردنەوەی خۆراوە ریب لە شتانە بەکەوە. لە هەندێک داتی

جۆرنژی ئادای کۆ بوونی مەسیح. شەرەبەتەی تەمامات. بەوە. تەنانەت بەریر پشتینی کوروس ی. تەوڵێت. کلینسی تەوڵێت بەریر لەوە بەکەوە نەوە. بەکەوە شیدوویلۆڵ هوڵمی فیلمی لە

ەیەنەاوەل    .ەوەنێهبریب تەوەڵمام ەیەناوەل ەناتاش مەئ نۆچ
یناەدرەس ۆب اهنەت    .ەوەتیزۆدب شی کەیەکۆرف ەل تۆخ
(نادێل ەڵپەچ .ساپوس . کەیەناخەکۆرف

6

# OXFORD PROPOSAL

In September 2019, it would be proposed that I would be invited to attend lectures at Wolfson College, a graduate level institution that is part of University of Oxford in the UK. As luck may have it, pandemic happened, and this was put on hiatus. However I wanted to include this section, with the hopes that through essays and other writing samples, included in subsequent editions, this story will be ongoing. For now, I offer this:

*Sample Itinerary in Oxford*

Day 1
Saturday, October 17
Travel day
Arrival in Oxford
Check in at Galaxie Hotel
Group dinner at
6 pm at Mamma Mia Pizzeria

Day 2
Sunday, October 18
Late morning guided boat tour – history and topography of Oxford
Included British Sunday late lunch at the Folley riverside restaurant
Free wandering in Oxford i.e. Blackwell's Books, Ashmoleon museum etc

Day 3
Monday, October 19
Walking tour of Oxford – history and monuments
Seminar with Dr. Kate Kennedy, OCLW, Wolfson College:
What is Life Writing?
Welcome tea

Day 4
Tuesday, October 20
Bodleian Library Registration and tour with archivist on collections relevant to course
OCLW evening lecture

Day 5
Wednesday, October 21
Morning Seminar – Sasha
Wolfson College
Research afternoon

Day 6
Thursday, October 22
On site lecture

OCLW evening lecture

Day 7
Friday, October 23
Morning seminar- Sasha
Research afternoon, early evening tour

Day 8
Saturday, October 24
Research Day

Day 9
Sunday, October 25
Afternoon cultural excursion- museum or theatre
Group dinner

Day 10
Monday, October 26
On site lecture
Afternoon seminar-Sasha

Day 11
Tuesday, October 27
On site lecture
OCLW event
Group dinner

Day 12
Wednesday, October 28
Mini-seminar and farewell breakfast
Return travel to Vancouver or stay in Oxford or independent

travel

# 7

# USER EXPERIENCE & SOPHOCLES

*i. Ideas trapped within us*

We have ideas within us. They swim through our minds and sometimes move faster than we know what to do with them. A young guy approached me after the event last night and asked me what to do, with all of these ideas he had in his head, that he had no way of keeping track of and communicating to anyone, let alone having them resonate in a way that he could start picking them apart. Ideas trapped within us is the idea that we are all a bit like this, bubbles for ideas that kind of swim around inside of us, and the keyhole that we have to unlock is getting those ideas out. By showing a slide of a person writing on a white board, I began to communicate an idea that we have ideas within us, and through a pen, the ideas can leave us and exist in the real world, through writing. It's simply writing, there's nothing special about it. Except for that fact that it is entirely special because it is a manifestation of our ideas. The ideas come out of us through writing and now they exist in the

physical world. And there is visibility on them.
*— And great wounds before today have taught sense even to the aged.... —* Sophocles, *Antigone*

## ii. Manifestation of ideas

In design, there is a notion of a maker. Maybe that person is a ceramics artist, maybe a construction worker, maybe an electrician, maybe a product designer. These people make real physical things that come into the world. Design legend John Maeda talks about the shift away from these craft based makers into a world where people do this through writing, sound, and code, a shift away from the maker. However I don't see this as a shift. I see writing, sound, and code as forms of making as well. Sure, they aren't what we ordinarily see as making, because we are making transient things, abstract things, but they are things and they are coming into the world and they exist within us before existing in the world and this process, this transfer is something I call Manifestation of ideas.
*For their grand schemes or bold words the proud pay with great wounds.... —* Sophocles, *Antigone*

## iii. Iteration

Recently I spoke at the TEDx conferences in Canada at Emily Carr University of Art + Design. I was in the first half, and before the second half we all assembled in the corridor to chat. I was in a group of three people. I was there, as a speaker, as a container for all these ideas running through my head about the talk, about how to memorize, how to internalize, how to be authentic, and of course how to be true to the content I was presenting. Beside me in this group of three was a young woman who was also a speaker, and I imagine had similar ideas inside her, and there was a third person, a guest at the event, who I imagine had all sorts of questions, and thoughts and feedback about the first half of the talks, and the three of us broke into conversation. And in the conversation a Manifestation of ideas was happening. I had my ideas leave my body, I was making, but not at all in the traditional sense because the ideas I was making were sonic, they were sound, they were leaving my body through voice. But they were ideas that were within me and they were then in the physical world, so in a sense I was making. But after that something happened. The ideas were listened to, reflected on, responded to, and then I grabbed the new ideas from the others, and then proceeded to make more ideas. To communicate new ideas. To manifest new ideas. But these ideas weren't just inside me and leaving me. These were ideas based on the ideas of others. So I was speaking my ideas, getting new ideas from the others, and then speaking more new ideas. And this process is iterative, and it's cyclical. Ideas are made, and then new ideas are made, and then new ideas are made again, over and over with perhaps the only restriction being an amount of time – time, we have to iterate on our ideas, to generate new ideas.

*To be sensible and to be pious are the first and last of happiness....*
— Sophocles, *Antigone*


*iv. Coming into the world through writing*


Back to Bangalore, I was sitting at a roundtable as a panelist with other design educators. They all have brown skin except me.  Top people at universities around India, and we were chatting. There were eight or ten of us at the table, and we were sharing out ideas. We were making. We were doing Manifestation of Ideas. But there were eight or ten of us there, so a huge amount of complexity. I'm sharing my ideas through voice at first, and then listening to eight or ten others before iterating, before saying more new ideas through voice. And then a third impartial person pulled out some paper on an easel, and starting writing our ideas down. So now the ideas are coming into the world through voice and writing, and they are coming into the world through iteration. So lo's of complexity, but again we are just making through conversation and writing stuff down, so hugely simple. And arguably not even qualifiable as making.

*You honour higher than all others, here, where lightning was your father. Now that a violent sickness holds the nation and all its people, come, over the slope of Parnassos, over the groaning channel, walk here and heal us. —* Sophocles, *Antigone*

*v. Coming into the world through speech*

And back to Canada. 29 audience members, preparing for the workshop portion of our evening which I have to run. "Have any of you been to Creative Mornings?" I ask. People pair up and turn their chairs towards one another and begin the session. The rules are minimal. One person represents a product and one person represents a user. I suggest one person is Siri and another is the user of Siri. Conversations begin. Great energy in the room. It's working. I set my timer on my iPhone for ten minutes. And time ticks down. People are talking. People are making.

*Sun-blaze, shining at last, you are the most beautiful light ever shown Thebes over her seven gates; and now, higher, widening gaze of gold day, you come, over the course of our west river. In whole armour Come out of argos (his shield shone white) you have expelled the man, exiled in unbridled and blinding flight. Out of the crisis of dubious quarrel Polynieces had roused him against our country. As shrill as an eagle on wings white as snow he flew onto the country, feathered in armour.* — Sophocles, *Antigone*

## vi. Our current technology

So wait, pen and paper are technology? Professor Haig Armen at Emily Carr University of Art + Design convinced me of this. We had an open house day and an older man came into the interaction lab, feathers in a mess, and asked what all this is. I scrambled. I pulled out a chair and said "You see what I did, I just pulled out a chair. There's a huge amount of complexity there that we don't see. We need the chair and me to pull it out, but the way in which I pull it out, the support from the chair to enable me to perform that action is the route of interaction". Haig jumps in. "Industrial Design is the making of the chair, the ergonomics, the health factor, or the human factors as we call them – making the chair just right for people. But Interaction design is something else." Haig and I have conflicting views and the old man tries to pick us apart. But he sees what we are saying. This is about people. And our technology these days is only at all relevant through people. And understanding people. *Your devotion is a kind of reverence. Power, though, must be revered, not trampled by those who must wield it.* — Sophocles, *Antigone*

## vii. Pen and paper

So now we know, pen and paper are technology. Why wouldn't they be? Many support the myth that complex digital things are technology. Or the VCR that we never learnt how to use is technology. Technology is impossible. Technology is difficult. You need to be smart to use technology... it's false. Technology enables. Pen and paper is one example, but pen and paper are actually quite complex, we can go even more simple.

*You were harsh and daring, child. You went too far and fell broken against the lofty pedestal of Justice. Perhaps, though, you are paying for some ancestral failing.* — Sophocles, *Antigone*, p. 54

*viii. Design by committee*

There is a phrase, too many cooks in the kitchen, that is now truer than ever within user experience. These days we see a rise in what we call user experience research, which is basically bringing a lot of people into a room with a lot of different backgrounds and together, they generate new and interesting ideas. People butt heads. Arguments ensue. No one wants to solve this. And design becomes a myth about how designers make more problems than they solve.

*Desire, you, unconquered war; Desire, vaulting upon dear goods; at night you rest on young girls smiles, then travel, grazing the deep ocean, to visit the far dwellers whose houses are fields. The deathless gods cannot escape, or humans whose whole life is a day. Welcoming you, they run mad.* — Sophocles, *Antigone*

*ix. Visibility*

Ten or 15 years ago I joined the dot com era with my first job title that included the words "User Experience." What was this "User Experience," I wondered. And why was I uniquely qualified to do it. I went into work everyday. Booted my Mac up. Made some stuff in Photoshop. Talked to my product manager. Had meetings. Lots of meetings. Then one day user experience happened. And I'll tell you how it happened – There is a thing called JIRA, which keeps track of tickets. Computer Science people who code all day make JIRAs whenever there is a problem, and the JIRA pops up on everyone's computer saying what the problem is. And everyone is like hmm. Interesting. At first a couple JIRAS are there, and then there are lots of JIRAS, and then there are a shit ton of JIRAS. The house is on fire now. We gotta do something about these JIRAS. And so we have a meeting. Great group of people, I know this because someone breaks the mould, writes his JIRA on a sticky note, and puts it up on the wall. "We're gonna do this with our JIRAS. We're gonna put them all on the wall, so we can all see them." That's when I learnt about visibility. All these ideas that exist are made visible. It was that day I learnt what I signed up for. User Experience was this visibility.

*Lucky those whose lifetime knows no trouble. The house quaked by the gods lacks no form of disaster creeping after all the clan; like swellings of ocean, when evil north winds breathe, that run on the abyss of brine and roll black sand up from the chasm – and headlands beat them back but bellow, wailing, wind-worn.* — Sophocles, *Antigone*


*x. Role Play*


And so, ta-da, I am certified in Role Play. Wait, what? It's okay, most people don't know what it means. In fact, I am still wrestling with what it means. However, I entered a room in Bangalore and left certified. More than that though, I left with purpose. The purpose or impetus to bring this idea back to Canada. So a couple of nights ago I'm in front of a room of 30 User Experience people, and they're like, "What is this Role Play", and everyone's feathers are in a mess. I scramble. Pass around a mic. and one person jumps up. "I do role play at work!" I'm right. I have evidence. Stress subsides. Now everyone is talking. Everyone is doing role play. I run the role play workshop in two parts. In both parts there were a pair of participants, one person was the product and one was the user. And the two talk to each other. For the second part, I introduce technologies – one person is the user and one person is iOS, or one person is the user and one person is Alexa. They talk to each other. Now times up. Now we act it in front of everyone. It's working.

*The breath of his life he has taught to be language, be the spirit of thought; griefs, to give laws to nations; fears, to dodge weapons of rains and winds and the homeless cold – always clever, he never fails to find ways for whatever future; manages cures for the hardest maladies; from death alone he has secured no refuge.* — Sophocles, *Antigone*


*xi. No Fidelity*


Complex digital products like Adobe Creative Suite and Raspberry Pi Operating systems, where you input commands using command line or weld together electronics, feel like they are authentically true ways of making things. And that making, at that level, is a level of fidelity. And often, we want to be just like this – as real as possible when trying out things, when prototyping things, so we up-and-up-and-up the level of fidelity. We start fairly low and we up-and-up and-up the fidelity. But what happens when we go the other way. What happens when we reduce the fidelity. Did you ever think of how complex, how much fidelity there is in a conversation. Yes, it's just two people talking, but people have the ideas, and are speaking the ideas, there is a time element, so people are constrained by the amount of time they can speak, and the amount of time allotted for the duration of the conversation, and these bits and bobs are things we are entirely reliant on. What if a person can't speak. Well, that ends it right there. But thats what we are dealing with here. Because there is no such thing as No fidelity. Because no matter how much you reduce and reduce and reduce the parameters, the limitations, the components that we are allowed to use, we are always left over with something. Something has to be there. And that something is a very, very low fidelity.

*Many marvels walk through the world, terrible, wonderful, but none more than humanity, which makes a way under winter rain, over the grad deep of the sea, proceeds where it swells and swallows; that grinds at the earth — unwinding, unwearied, first of the gods– to its own purpose as the plow is driven turning year into year, through generations as colt follows mare.* — Sophocles, *Antigone*

*xii. Top down*

Alas, Bangalore. Bangalore all over again. I'm at the roundtable discussion again. "Bottom up!" I say. I know what I'm talking about. I've heard it from powerless people. They have good ideas. And those ideas need to be heard. That's what bottom-up is. "But India is an emerging market" they insinuate "And we are people of power. Let's make rules for our people. This is what they crave. Rules." The conference ends. I come back to Vancouver with top down mentality in mind, but I'm sceptical. "What do you mean by top down and bottom up?" the audience member in Canada asks me at my talk. "How do we get there". Shit. Another unsolvable problem. A wicked problem. A feedback loop. I'm stifled "Bottom-up!" I say again. I feel like Hitler. or Trump. "Bottom-up Bottom-up Bottom-up Bottom-up!" Maybe if I repeat myself something will happen.

*Zeus hates the noise of a bragging tongue. When he saw them come against us in a great gush, grandiose with splashing gold, he whirled fire; and the man who was rushing like a racer to the goal on the heights of our battlements and was signalling victory, Zeus hurled him down with that fire.* — Sophocles, *Antigone*


*xiii. Prototyping Workshop*


Empowering young designers or tech people or students, is what I aim to do. And if I do that then I've succeeded. There are many ways to do things that benefit myself, and one might argue that empowering people by giving them my ideas, is a form of retaining power. If I was capable of such malevolence, I would probably be much better off. But I'm just a guy with some ideas so let's start and end there. Or in sum, this paper describes an impetus I had, after travelling to India, to return to Canada and share my ideas. These ideas resemble a kind of bricolage of ideas on the page, a loose terms of agreement for a reader so they can say "We learnt that. It's real."

*Victory comes bringing glory to Thebes, answers a smile to our many chariots that cheer her. Now that the war is over, forget war. We'll visit every god's temples, for a whole night, dancing and chanting praise. Dionysus leads us, rules Thebes, makes the land tremble. —*

Sophocles, *Antigone*

# 8

# POETIC MODALITY

*Ghandi Airport*

*Night was day when I arrived in Delhi,*
*at Ghandi.*
*I packed safely, but quickly found my water bottle missing as I*
*pushed through the crowd*
*and approached a Delhi walla.*
*My eyes adjusted.*
*I tried to get a read but all I could see*
*was a tattered collared polo and waving and shouting and brown*
*skin. Jet lag*
*hit hard as I got in the taxi,*
*the ambassador taxi.*
*I had given up. I just wanted out of*
*that mess.*
*I transited through Shanghai. My ex-wife was there.*
*We started driving and the screaming and shouting fanned off.*
*I wondered how*
*he could pretend he knew where we were going. "Delhi is big you*

*know?”*
*India is big, he meant.*
*Eventually we pulled up and I went in.*
*“Can I help you?”*
*The friendly voice behind the desk.*
*It occurred to me it was some sort of Internet cafe.*
*I shoved him over and typed some words into his personal computer.*
*“Hotel. Delhi. New Rajendra Nagar”*
*“This one!”*
*We eventually did arrive that night.*
*What seemed like big wins that first week*
*at the hotel were not.*
*Walking one block in either direction of the hotel.*
*Eating sparsely from the hotel buffet.*
*Learning the hotel wifi password.*
*It was hot and I was sweating.*
*I desperately wanted to do laundry.*
*Some emails came through about the class*
*I was supposed to start teaching,*
*I quickly clicked through them.*
*I ordered more bottled water.*
*The HR, Punita came to pick me up*
*with her husband some mornings later.*
*She came to greet me in the small lobby of the hotel*
*and we walked out to the car.*
*Full of energy I was whisked off*
*to the college gates*
*where we drove onto the college grounds.*
*I*
*was*
*home.*

*Vasant Kunj*

*When I put water to my face black soot exfoliated.*
*I shouldn't be walking outside.*
*I had heard a story of colleagues getting exercise*
*by walking around shopping malls.*
*I hopped in a rickshaw*
*and about an hour later was dropped off way outside the city.*
*That's where I discovered*
*Vasant Kunj.*
*Vasant Kunj was a district with three shopping malls and a hotel.*
*The first mall was quite nice and familiar.*
*Nike.*
*Levis.*
*Body Shop.*
*It felt like home.*
*Through a courtyard that first mall connected to a second mall.*
*Diesel.*
*Tiffany's.*
*Okay this was a bit nicer.*
*Then you transited to the third mall.*
*The third mall*
*was where I spent most of my time.*
*I had a routine in the third mall.*
*I usually ordered 3 different muffins with marmalade and butter,*
*a good strong Americano,*
*and a spot where I looked around at people looking at me,*
*who in turn looked at each other.*
*It was a bit awkward*
*but when I returned home my mouth wasn't caked with dust,*
*and I could in a way forget that it was*

*45C*
*and I was in India,*
*which was a good thing at that time.*
*I bought socks at Paul Smith*
*and walked into*
*Diesel Gold*
*where they greeted me as Mr. Girard.*

*Vasant Vihar*

*Mariangela lived in Vasant Vihar,*
*a diplomatic neighbourhood*
*with green trees and quiet side streets.*
*One evening after a stint at the expat grocery store*
*we made chicken soup*
*from a Martha Stewart recipe.*
*Mariangela had a cold*
*and it seemed like the obvious thing to do.*
*She lit candles on the terrace*
*while I checked on the broth.*
*"Should I book the Meru cab?"*
*I served the broth made with chicken breast and relaxed for a bit.*
*The mosquito coils*
*gave off a swizzle*
*of smoke*
*as well as aroma.*
*The whole thing felt spiritual.*
*I wondered if it was.*
*The flat at Vasant Vihar*
*sat on top of a modest house.*
*Mariangela*

*informed me that she had to get someone to carry up the water*
*cooler*
*to the rooftop,*
*and that it was probably made for a housekeeper*
*as I walked through and adorned the Indian style furniture*
*and collection of sculptural conversation pieces,*
*along with*
*Ikea necessities.*
*There was no*
*Ikea*
*in New Delhi yet. I propped open my 13 inch*
*MacBook Air*
*so we could watch*
*Oblivion, my favourite New Delhi discovery.*
*I liked Tom Hanks charm.*

*Khan Market*

*Amici*
*was in Khan Market*
*and part of my self imposed diet items was a margarita pizza and a*
*fresh lime soda mixed,*
*so I haggled over rupees*
*with the*
*auto rickshaw driver*
*so I could get down there.*

9

# NON-POETIC MODALITY

*Lecturer, New Delhi*

*Ghandi Airport*

Night was day when I arrived in Delhi, at Ghandi.  I packed safely, but quickly found my water bottle missing as I pushed through the crowd and approached a Delhi walla.  My eyes adjusted. I tried to get a read but all I could see was a tattered collared polo and waving and shouting and brown skin. Jet lag hit hard as I got in the taxi, the ambassador taxi. I had given up. I just wanted out of that mess.

I transited through Shanghai. My ex-wife was there.

We started driving and the screaming and shouting fanned off. I wondered how he could pretend he knew where we were going. "Delhi is big you know?" India is big he meant.

Eventually we pulled up and I went in.

"Can I help you?" The friendly voice behind the desk. It occurred to me it was some sort of Internet cafe. I shoved him over and typed some words into his personal computer. "Hotel. Delhi. New Rajendra Nagar"

"This one!" Eureka. We were on our way?

We eventually did arrive that night. What seemed like big wins that first week at the hotel were not. Walking one block in either direction of the hotel. Eating sparsely from the hotel buffet. Learning the hotel wifi password. It was hot and I was sweating. I desperately wanted to do laundry. Some emails came through about the class I was supposed to start teaching, I quickly clicked through them. I ordered more bottled water.

The HR, Punita came to pick me up with her husband some mornings later. She came to greet me in the small lobby of the hotel and we walked out to the car. Full of energy I was whisked off to the college gates where we drove onto the college grounds. I was home.

*Vasant Kunj*

When I put water to my face black soot exfoliated. I shouldn't be walking outside. I had heard a story of colleagues getting exercise by walking around shopping malls. I hopped in a rickshaw and about an hour later was dropped off way outside the city. That's where I discovered Vasant Kunj. Vasant Kunj was a district with three shopping malls and a hotel. The first mall was quite nice and familiar. Nike. Levis. Body Shop. It felt like home. Through a courtyard that first mall connected to a second mall. Diesel. Tiffany's. Okay this was a bit nicer. Then you transited to the third mall. The third mall was where I spent most of my time.

I had a routine in the third mall. I usually ordered 3 different muffins with marmalade and butter, a good strong Americano, and a spot where I looked around at people looking at me, who in turn looked at eachother. It was a bit awkward but when I returned home my mouth wasn't caked with dust, and I could in a way forget that it was 45C and I was in India, which was a good thing at that time. I bought socks at Paul Smith and walked into Diesel Gold where they greeted me as Mr. Girard.

*Vasant Vihar*

Mariangela lived in Vasant Vihar, a diplomatic neighborhood with green trees and quiet side streets. One evening after a stint at the expat grocery store we made chicken soup from a Martha Stewart recipe. Mariangela had a cold and it seemed like the obvious thing to do. She lit candles on the terrace while I checked on the broth. "Should I book the Meru cab?" I served the broth made with chicken breast and relaxed for a bit. The mosquito coils gave off a swizzle of smoke as well as aroma. The whole thing felt spiritual. I wondered if it was.

The flat at Vasant Vihar sat on top of a modest house. Mariangela informed me that she had to get someone to carry up the water cooler to the rooftop, and that it was probably made for a housekeeper as I walked through and adorned the Indian style furniture and collection of sculptural conversation pieces, along with Ikea necessities. There was no Ikea in New Delhi yet. I propped open my 13 inch MacBook Air so we could watch Oblivion, my favorite New Delhi discovery. I liked Tom Hanks charm.

*Khan Market*

Amici was in Khan Market and part of my self imposed diet items was a margarita pizza and a fresh lime soda mixed, so I haggled over rupees with the auto rickshaw driver so I could get down there. Stray dogs approached but the autorickshaw drivers at Khan Market were the real culprits. They knew they could charge whatever they wanted and handed together to do so. We got in the habit of walking a couple of blocks into the middle of nowhere when we were ready to leave so we wouldn't have to deal with them. "Chaiwalla!" I debated grabbing some tea on the side of the street on arrival before approaching the labyrinth of shops and more shops. I could never remember which alley I had to go down to get to Amici. Mariangela accompanied me and sometimes Chloe and we would sit and chat and eat pizza and wipe the sweat from our foreheads. There wasn't much else to do, but we didn't need much - we were just happy to be away from the filth on the streets. I debated trying to find the latest Monocle magazine next week, a couple months old on arrival but one of my only antennas receiving news from outside India. I took a refill of my drink.

*Haus Khas Village*

The iPad has just come out and Mariangela was using it as

a GPS mapping device to make sure the autorickshaw was on the right track. She would scream at the driver when he made a wrong turn and eventually face palmed when she realized she had no control over where the driver was going.  It was hot and there weren't many options.  Haus Khas Village was hard to find but skirting down the narrow road, you wouldn't know it with the Woodstock like arrival. Dilapidated buildings connected overhead, it was a kind of high school gymnasium for adults, a place to drink and chat and whatever else. I brought my MacBook one time and pulled my way up what I originally thought was a vanity staircase onto a rooftop terrace where I had an ice with coke and grabbed the phone for Mariangela to meet me. She was there in a few minutes and I was puzzled how she found it. "Are you just gonna spend your whole Saturday here" Mariangela was from Milano, Italy and had no shame wearing her culture on her sleeve, screaming her language at the Indians. I tried to calm her down.

*Sharpujat*

Everyone talked about Sharpujat but no one had actually been there. I was teaching interaction design but I was at a fashion design school, and all the lecturers shared stories about getting fabric died there, checking out the studios of up and coming designers, finding studio space and being a bit under the radar there.  Chloe motioned me onto a rickshaw one day to go there. It lived up. We walked through the crumbling alleys and half renovated designer spaces, past villagers dying in bright coloured buckets and sewing machine factories spitting out an almost imperceptible hum through the hole on the wall windows.  "This way" she said.  We had an appointment to see a space that she was interested in converting into a maker space. "No check this out". The noise of the alleys dimmed as we found our way into a beautiful completely redone space with high end renovations and matching garment price tags. I was offered a drink and Chloe sorted through the bins, more for ideas than anything else.

*Agra*

It was 2013 and the high speed expressway connecting Delhi and Agra was finally nearing completion. I was hearing stories about how the brave and ambitious had bipassed the blockades and made the trip, only really lacking shops and amenities that might exist along the way after a formal opening. My students expressed interest in making a travel study out of it, so we packed ourselves in a Honda one early morning and began. I was seduced at the time of it being a "spiritual journey" and dealt with a lot of kickback from my students for calling it that. But I didn't care. I brought the college DSLR and a couple large memory cards with me, and pretty quickly asked to pull over alongside a readying truck to shoot some video. The 48 hour film festival was accepting submissions and I wanted to submit. The camera switched itself off after 30 seconds. "Spiritual journey!" Rao mocked. He was a budding film maker and knew I was extremely underprepared. We both more or less ignored eachother and did our own thing, knowing that our lack of collaboration was going to hinder us both. "Check this out" I motioned him over to look at the raw footage. "Do you think we can use this?" Fast forward to mid-trip, I was asleep in the back seat after talking incessantly and not having enough coffee. I don't remember a single bump or glitch during that sleep, only being awoken suddenly. "We're here" I looked out the window and saw a Paul cafe. They meant a place to get coffee at. I quickly went back to sleep. All I really remember about how that trip unfolded was that I never made it to the Tag Mail, instead opting to sleep in the lounge of the radisson blue waiting for my students to come get me. I might have found my way to the hotel buffet for a big breakfast but mostly I was just sleeping. I think I preferred the trip that way anyways.

*Rajasthan*

I didn't have an exorbitant salary as a university lecturer but one month when my deposit hit my account I realized I could go buy a Canon DSLR camera and still scrape by that month on mostly Dhal from the school cafeteria. I went to Crystal Mall and grabbed a camera body, SD card, flash and a couple of 50 1.2 lenses and was feeling pretty good. I decided to make a research project out of it and began booking a trip to the pink city, Jaipur. I wanted to see if it was really pink. "Will you come" I asked Mariangela. I was eyeing a walled garden hotel on trip advisor, a kind of retreat space where you didn't have to look at the real Rajasthan. We could eat well and chill in the garden and then venture out with the camera when it was time to eat the soot and the grit. I blew up a picture at London Drugs Photo years later of migrant workers in the back of a truck shot from my taxi window. "This. This is what I want to shoot" we were grid locked and had nothing to look at except the community of monkeys that occupied the rooftops of a derelict residential neighborhood in the middle of nowhere "We might have to come back for that" alas we never did.

*Pink City*

It was less pink, more like the colour palette of the meaty half of a moderately priced chakutury board.  It started to depress me and I wanted to go back to the hotel, only stopping in one main neighborhood to walk through and quickly shoot a hundred or so photo from the hip of whatever my camera would grab.  Later I would teach a digital photography class at the college where we would go into a neighborhood in old Delhi and shoot from the hip exactly the same way. Hiring a car and driver wasn't expensive and I wanted the camera anyway so I wasn't particularly disappointed, and tried to arrange the photo editing in the view finder and wondering if I had anything there.

# 10

# BOOK REVIEWS

*Things We Could Design: For More Than Human-Centered Worlds*
*by Ron Wakkary*
*Cambridge, MA: MIT Press 2021*
*$35.00 (US) / 9780262542999*

Ron Wakkary's Things We Could Design: For More Than Human-Centered Worlds is a delightful book that brings us into an important conversation taking place in Vancouver, Canada, and beyond. Although one might call this a conversation about design, and yes, interactive design, it's really something else entirely. And it's something you all need to know about.

To begin, you might learn that Vancouver is divided into streams of thought in the interactive world, and one of those more academic streams is at Simon Fraser University's School of Interactive Arts and Technology. Through long lists of citations, tenured professors, PhD candidates, suburban campuses, and funded research labs we begin to discover that there's a whole world of knowledge here. If we were to call this design, we might know that design as a dinner table conversation perhaps ordinarily manifests thought bubbles of a perfectly ergonomic chair or a dating app that actually works.

But what goes on behind this? Ron Wakkary brings us into those conversations ranging from design and the Anthropocene to design for non-human animals. He brings an almost imperceptible hum to the machinery that affords a lucky few of us a way of life. His journey becomes our and your journey, and quite quickly you start to ask, "Did I get this?" and "Wait! what?" before flipping to the next chapter in eager anticipation. Like me, you might find Things We Could Design sitting by your bedside table, with rereads being equally fruitful.

In reference to the specifics of design terminology, in what we might call Ron's world, the interactive speaks to all of us especially in the way we use things, the way we like things, the reasons we use things, and the possibilities we create by using things. Where names like Moggridge and Norman end, Wakkary begins. Wakkary creates opportunities and solves problems about the interactive in Things We Could Design mainly by supporting a traditionally practice-based field that prides itself in contributing practical design knowledge to any layperson. But it could be argued that his particular angle is on the theoretical ramp or approach. And this is still quite new: the idea that, through theory, design can make progress and start to co-create and be generative in ways that incorporate ideas from other somewhat tangential fields. One actual gap that's addressed here, if we wanted to venture a bit, is that perhaps design can be entirely in our heads, and still make headway.

Climate, political views, space travel, and autonomous cars are very much design things, both in practice and in theory, and Wakkary reveals this by being boldly implicit and delicate.

If you're interested in the contemporary everyday silos of design, you might populate your palette with words like user experience, graphic design, colours, fonts, etc., especially when making reference to the interactive. Things We Could Design is a bit more than that. But what it helps us understand is important: that we can all participate in bigger ideas and conversations of design and that we can all, in a way, be its practitioners. A lifetime of studies in the area might help, and sometimes we think we can't compete with those holding appropriate degree qualifications, but you'll soon understand that a degree frame of mind limits you at the same time, because you no longer have access to "fresh eyes," the seeing of a thing for the first time, the point of view that researchers in the area so desperately seek out and create room and empathy for.

Ron Wakkary's book represents the nodes of a worldview expressed at Simon Fraser University's School of Interactive Arts and Technology. On the one hand it might seem heavy, but more importantly it provides access to a wealth and breadth of knowledge that the academy supports. Things We Could Design is deep, beautiful, and a little quirky. For the layperson wanting entry into another world, where thought and imagination in all of its modalities are king, this book is for you. You'll find it at the same time as precious as it is contextual, representing a piece of our time that is very much needed and too seldom released for the masses.

I would include it on the very top of my short stack of relevant books and I think you should too, if only to say, "I know that one. And I liked it."

*Art + DIY Electronics*
*by Garnet Hertz*
*Cambridge, MA: The MIT Press, May 30, 2023*
*$45.00 / 9780262044936 (paperback)*

Dr. Garnet Hertz new book on DIY culture – Art + DIY Electronics– is a refreshing change from typical academic texts. It has the heft, but without the intimidation of a work that appears as if it requires too much heavy lifting. It qualifies itself, bringing in sources and reference material that are inspiring, but also appropriate, yet it does it with a literary narrative quality that makes you want to read it. With my review copy, at first glance, I was intimidated. As I skimmed the pages deciding how I was going to sink my teeth in, I learnt that it was possible to skim it. I stopped now and then checking out the vibrant, diverse, inclusive images and engaging captions. I was sold: sold not on the idea that I could just skim it, but sold on the idea that I could and would want to return to it and all its parts, again and again. I was sold enough that I could eventually perhaps risk myself in saying it would enter my scholastic vocabulary.

Let me be clear: this was not my first introduction to Garnet's work. We had chatted about his most recent skate park work, documenting and creating graffiti at a local skate park after work – after putting in the time in his prestigious and hon-ourable appointment at Emily Carr University of Art and Design.

We had talked about other artists doing similar things in similar places these days, notably artist Germaine Koh who is also in the DIY space in a way. We had talked about what he loves with his work, things like risograph printing, zines, and "making" in all forms. But we hadn't dug in in the way this book does even at first glance, showing that he does the heavy lifting behind the ideas that you might think he just passes off in conversation, without really knowing. Let me be clear: he knows this stuff.

If I'm risking being too meta or contextual, I will anyway and say or acknowledge that this is an important work for this artist and academic. Garnet has certainly been anticipating and preparing for the release of this book. If you follow his everyday process, he is often talking informally about how he has been preparing to invest himself in the marketing and speaking about a book of this nature. He doesn't shy away from the reality that this book is a key piece in his academic journey, which only stops now and then for things like Fulbright recognition and a Canada Research Chair appointment. Garnet is at the top of his game and yet this book is an important milestone for him.

At first glance, I noted the inclusion of references from India. I had already become acquainted with a school called Srishti in Bangalore, and was delighted to see it mentioned with pairing imagery in even a glance of the book. That was because it was not the only reference to other places. This work could have easily made its way through the appropriate content without sharing topics that might be other. It doesn't take that often-taken safety net, and instead says 'let's include that, even highlight and care about that,' perhaps to say it is inspiring for young academic readers who can now say even academic books these days care and invite change in the world.

There are few books that I care enough to read thoroughly in the academic realm of the art, design, and humanities spaces. This is one. It highlights the necessary materials for people with checklists and boxes to tick, but it does it in a deeply caring way. It has a kind of subtle humour that makes you want to meet the author. It is warm and familiar, and beautiful, and different enough that even if you wanted to get the material somewhere else, you wouldn't be able to. But I'm certain, you wouldn't want to anyway. This book aspires to be the authoritative text in this aspect of the DIY space, and with that it succeeds. But it is more than that, it is a human text, and that's a value that needs a checkbox so badly: a checkbox that this book fills with every pencil, pen, and heart.

Enjoy it, I did.

*Pretty Pictures*
*by Marian Bantjes*
*New York: Metropolis Books, 2013*
*$99.00 / 9781938922220*

I know of Marian Bantjes through folklore growing up studying design. The story goes that she was a print production craftsperson / typesetter / grunt work employee until one day later in life she started hanging out on an Internet forum, in the '90s, trying to break into the design elite, and through that channel became looped in with the names of the day, and specifically Stefan Sagmeister, who eventually started handing her spillover work from agencies. She resides on a small island near Vancouver. But it's through Pretty Pictures that we see that there was more to her story in her remote location, in terms of the skill and craft of a designer that obviously had gifts beyond an ability to network or luck into her status.

The first thing you'll notice is the sheer heft of this book. Like books by designers in the '60s and '70s, this thing is massive, and beautiful. Instantaneously you'll know where your money went. It's a big book. The contents are quite simply page after page of beautiful intricate ornamentation – typographic niceties that make you think it's AI generated, only to later realize this work precedes modern AI. The writing is typeset creatively, with ping pong paragraphs flexing in and out of columns and column wraps. You might not read it, but you'll definitely notice it, and surely remember it. Flipping through in Pinterest fashion appears to be encouraged, and as you do it images might be conjured of black turtleneck minimalism architecture graphic design studio creatives working on the next big thing. You might step away only to return minutes or hours later for another dose.

Few people have done work in this realm simply because it's so time consuming and difficult to master, I imagine. The names of the typographic world can be associated with movements: April Greiman with postmodernism, Jessica Hische with lettering, Matthew Carter with typeface design, and for the most part they go unchallenged. I would say Bantjes through this book does that with typographic ornamentation. There is no one who is her equal in this respect.

One notable aspect of Bantjes typographic compositions is that they all resemble the poster. The poster is a hallmark of typography and perhaps one deliverable that will never disappear. But in fact, Bantjes work crosses over many deliverables, most obviously print and the printed poster, but also digital and screen-based work. It's tangential to mention it, but one might simply take a look at the graphic compositions she is currently making using AI and Mid Journey to say that perhaps she has switched modalities. But the truly timeless modalities – books, posters, lettering – these always seem to poke their heads out in the work of great designers, especially as we move across time and so it wouldn't be surprising to hear assumptions that Bantjes will always remain in some ways in the typographic realm. Pretty Pictures, old but not collecting dust, predates a lot of these observations but is interesting to look at for any budding designer considering possibilities for the future.

This type of book is Pinterest before Pinterest, a way of gathering inspiration when it was primarily an arduous task. The physicality is something that can never be discounted, and I imagine the authors of the future will continue to always refer to books like this, as nothing quite replaces the ah-ha experience of leafing through it and coming to know to things in an unexplainable way, like a dream guiding you in the middle of the night.

In some respects, her work is flat-out timeless, as much as it is a product of a certain time, era, genre, modality, status... a product of history one might say. Experience the ephemera of the printed page, and a passage through time.

# 11

# TYPOGRAPHY ESSAYS

*History of Typography*

It would be hard to discount typography without first address-ing its roots in the way we live.  I was first drawn to the design history reference of stone tablets being carved into with lettering, and that lettering, at the very beginning, at least according to Megg's, being about finance – about recording the ownership of things. Because it goes back that far, you have to start in a way by saying, 'okay, this is significant.' The printing press is another obvious example. If you're learning textbook graphic design you might draw reference to the Gutenberg Bible, a massively reproduced manifestation of ideas, to say the least, or the Kelmscott Press, and the intricacies of hand-drawn typographic ornamentation on books, on borders of pages, and so on. Because these were so every day, so ubiquitous at least in the realm of these particular deliverables, and so important in the transfer of language throughout time, we, in a way, must continue this belief that these are important. Again, it's very difficult to discount typography in this realm as a passage through time.

Finally, we start to hit the digital age, and talk about people being more playful with type: people like April Greiman saying typography can exist on the computer, people like Zuzana Licko with Emigre Type Foundry, saying that these typographic cards are not set in stone, they can be played with, they can transition out of what we could call design modernism, into postmodernism, and then beyond that all the way into the small screens that we carry around. At that point, typography becomes undeniably key; a historical monument. The discussion becomes proven regardless of how you might argue for or against it.

*The interpretation of typography*

Where we get into debate is around how typography can be so important if we don't talk about it that much. Perhaps that's the area we need to work on the most, in terms of typography as dinner table conversation, in terms of the use of Helvetica being of serious everyday debate, in terms of typography being outside the realm of time, outside the realm of possibly going extinct. It cannot. It is to be always relevant. So we enter into our everyday, let's just say, extremely consequential uses of it, which prove its point and point out its state of being underrepresented.

*Where typography is going*

Where we're arriving at is that typography is more consequential than ever, regardless of if we notice it or not. So, let's notice it. The design of an election ballot, the design of highway signage with typefaces like DIN or Clearview or some variation chosen by the engineer of the day, resulting in the life and death of people who rely on it. They rely on it for those everyday, consequential, life or death choices. The pill bottle inscribed with typography that dictates the medication you may or may not take, to decide the length of your life. The signage you notice fast enough to make that critical turn correctly on the road. These decisions are typographic.

*Some examples*

We all love the names of fonts in shaping our understanding of typography so let's go there for a moment.

Gill Sans is, I think, common enough that we might know of it, or hear of it. It was designed by Eric Gill and being a very British typographic choice. It's most obviously noticed if you are in London or the surrounding areas and see its ubiquity, even today. And it's strange, because Eric Gill was not in any way an ordinary person but was responsible for the design of something that became so ordinary, yet in a way shouldn't have been because by many measures it is quite odd. Gill Sans is memorable in a way that I would argue goes against its readability, legibility, and ability to be popular in the most common form of typographic form, which is simply to be read.

Let's return to Helvetica, which in a mainstream way, perhaps, became popular in the 1970s when its massive corporate iden-tity application across the board made it part of almost every scene and background and physical environment. In many ways it shouldn't have done that because although it was considered to be clean, and efficient, and approachable, it was in fact, so much so, that it was not memorable. Its implementation dictated that it needed to be memorable. As a corporate device, Helvetica was to differentiate a lot of those corporate juggernauts and serve that specific memorable purpose.

In both these cases, we are faced with very well-designed typefaces, in a way going against the norm of how they should have played out in history – subverting themselves in terms of their obviousness, and becoming so popular that they were a different kind of everyday visual language.

*Where we enter*

Erik Spiekermann is one choice of entry into all this – a German typeface designer, and legend in many rights, that for many people made visible this profession. For typography, or let's say typeface design, he has been responsible for the passage of time. His type foundry is Fontshop, and has created a postmodern interpretation of Helvetica through FF Meta. His popular book Stop Stealing Sheep & Find Out How Type Works made bold statements around how letterspacing should and shouldn't be used by graphic designers of his time and this time. His proud, bold attitude compliments his life work and prepares us to take seriously what might most often be simply overlooked: typography. His necessity in the world of typography allows us to create a framework around other pieces of visual history that we might encounter. It might be Jan Tschichold's black, white, and red formulas or Wolfgang Weingart's chopped in half TYPOGRAPHY book cover lettering, or something more present day like the corporate Google Fonts, and their symphonies of Monserrat and Railway. And, of course, there's Apple's variants. Spiekermann was a coming of age for many, and his oddity was a calling to put our eyes on this profession much more than anyone was doing.

*Where we jump forward to*

Perhaps this is how we arrive. Artificial Intelligence (AI) is the conversation of present day, and in that conversation we need to talk about all of these references. Maybe that's AI's strength: to take all of the typographic knowledge that's been invested in and shape it and photograph it into the collages of digital space, into the technological worlds of AR and VR manifestation, regardless of if they are Meta or Apple or Amazon. The AI typographic calling can't be downplayed, in fact it must be up-played right now, at this pioneering time, so we can remember Helvetica, not for its 2007 film, but for its typeface/historical relevance, that put everything visual on the map for all of us and continues to do that today, and will continue to do that every day, as we move forward, propelled by typographic history or otherwise...

*Where is Type Going?*

A good way of looking at where type is going is to look at where it has been most recently. From Apple to Google, the big guns have made their presence known, and not necessarily tied it to the word typography, but there can be no doubt that that's exactly where it has been.

Talking about specifics of typeface choices in a world where even typographic choices like serifs, italics, and double spacing can seem daunting enough, is a challenge. But through engaging in Googling of words like typographic readability and legibility we can start to see how these choices make a difference, even to the least discerning eye that might be reading, as type casts its magic spell on you. After that, Google Fonts, Apple Fonts, and other more historical fonts and their type designers will become everyday ideas for you and you will be armed to go to battle with a heavy-duty typographic toolkit. In our overstimulated feeds and worlds of impression analytics, you'll be ready to fight the good fight, or help others with their aims as well.

Let's dive into a few examples.

*SF (San Francisco)*

SF is a font by Apple that made its way onto my radar while teaching interaction design at Emily Carr University of Art and Design on their certificate program. During that program the students had a small window to move outside of the conceptual, theoretical framework of study and start to play, and to play those days and in that place meant to play visually, and inevitably that meant to play with fonts.

For many years Apple had used, on iPhone, a variation of Helvetica that was pretty safe and reasonable, I thought. However, the phone came later, after Helvetica as inventions go, and so Helvetica at that time was in a way being repurposed for the phone, and the iPhone. You wouldn't know it at the time, as it seemed to work very well. Craftsman at Apple like interface designer Mike Matas made very good use of the visual tools of the day when creating visual interfaces for early iPhone, so at the very least in terms of usage of Helvetica, and how it seemed on the iPhone, well, it seemed very reasonable and very fitting. But, of course, Apple would have to consider that iPhone was going to need something more iconic for iPhone, as it became so ubiquitous. Apple was going to need a font that it could own, in the association with iPhone, and that perhaps it could span across more devices and tech and Apple products and services essentially, and so a new font had to be created in the shadow of Helvetica of that time period, and that font was SF.

When I first became aware of SF, I had probably seen it implemented already and didn't really notice the difference. I shouldn't admit that, as anyone who has a responsibility to have a typographic eye, should see the difference right away. But I didn't. But when I looked closely the difference between Helvetica and SF was probably that SF didn't look as well done. Some of the curves and glyphs seemed a bit wonky and kind of not right. And perhaps that's the way it had to be to work well on the devices, which it did, and still does. But it wasn't Helvetica. And as typographers and type designers throughout history have often noted, it's not easy to just remake Helvetica. Nothing can quite do that.

*NY (New York)*

I don't know NY as intimately as SF. I just found it, and found it obvious that SF by Apple needed a companion font, and NY was obviously that. It was a bit unexpected as it dropped. It's common for big names that are branded to create a font for themselves done by one of the top type designers. I often think of the font for Yale University done by Matthew Carter, a lifelong type master who created some great work at Microsoft Typography among a lot of great work in his lifetime. Yale was obviously a beautifully crafted, fitting, modern, but also academic typeface. It was as Yale as Yale could be in an innovative modern way. And Yale, the font, was it. There was no companion with a different name in the way that Apple had done. That's why what Apple did was so surprising. But maybe that's the sign of the times.

*Monserrat*

Google Fonts – which gets a lot of criticism by older designers, and a lot of fame and appreciation by younger designers, I think, because of its ability to be used easily and used well – was a necessary step forward in the type world. It has the big name Google attached to it but by many regards it could have been named something else, as long as it still had the ability to influence and become ubiquitous in the way that it did. Regardless of if you're talking about Monserrat or Raleway or Brandon Grotesque, you're talking about type of this era, type of user experience perhaps, type of slide decks perhaps, type of the necessary modern visual aesthetic, the look that we all know now, in the realm of places like flat design and everything after the long stretch of trying to use Helvetica for that purpose. Google Fonts really did the job and even if you tried to convince a young designer that decades of typography existed before and were the foundation for all of this, they might very well lean towards Google Fonts anyway, perhaps when you aren't looking or aren't noticing.  Even the older designers would perhaps turn their heads away in shame but also admit that it looks okay.  These days who can argue with that, especially when typography has begun to collect dust and fewer people have the luxury of spending the time necessary to become fully adjusted, and, let's say, good at typography.

It's hard to be good at typography. It's not hard to be good at Google Fonts.

*Minion*

Minion is a great, historical, beautiful, useful typeface.  But it wasn't until recently that I started seeing it in high end design for screens.  It was always a type for print, and type that you could pull up in Adobe Creative Cloud or Creative Suite before then and reliably use to make good work. I think I was looking at CMS (Content Management System) templates and saw this trend of using Minion. Perhaps I was recently looking at personal websites that were done by agencies and noticed Minion. I was pleased. Actually, to be fully disclosed, at first, I was like, "what is that font that they're using for screen in that way that looks so good" and only later uncovered that it was Minion. Minion to me will always be tied to Adobe CC and print design but I would say the way that it is being used these days on screen is probably the best I've ever seen it, and that's saying a lot as it's a beautiful, carefully-crafted typeface of the highest order. It is among a few of the, let's say, more recent typefaces that would actually fall into a designer's fistful-of-good-type toolkit, and we should all be happy that it's still around.

*Knockout*

Perhaps the one typeface, the one really good typeface, that doesn't really fall into an old or new category, is Knockout. You can click over to typography.com to see all the weights and usages of this one. Paula Scher of Pentagram at one point often mentioned Knockout as a go-to. It's elegant, beautiful, useful, and has managed to stay on the radar for years despite the influx of the Googles and Apples. It's a sans serif type, which seems to be a determining factor in choosing type these days. It isn't cheap, but there are worse things to buy than buying fonts, and through layouts and in-use examples you can pitch it to be expensed to a client.

Typeface selection is something that evolves over time, and is perhaps the most desirable knowledge to be had by a typographic layperson. It's useful, applicable, and takes us back into typeface history in a way that we want to know about it.

Hopefully, this entry gives you glimpse into what has been relevant for say the last decade, and will allow you to make better choices for you, your users, your clients, or whatever manifestations that you stumble upon. Type is a graphic designer's secret weapon, something only graphic designers know about, but it doesn't have to be that way. Entries like this can bring it into dinner table conversation and increasingly spread knowledge about this area of study. Type is only archaic and strange if we make it that way. In fact, it is very much something we can all talk about.

*Where We Enter*

Typography doesn't have one specific entry point anymore: it has many. If you're ready to up your game, let's look at a few here. Excuse the complexity of typographic language used here: typography is both an art and a science which makes complexity where it doesn't necessarily need to be. That's one of the dangers that we can puddle jump over, though. Typography and its people are the most normal part of this philosophical balloon, which is why we talk about it and them.

The names that find their way into these column entries are by no means exhaustive. Typography can be a place to enjoy for a lifetime, and many do spend their lives in this way. Today, typography can be approached in many different ways whereas at many times in history there was simply a single story and single entry point. Choosing whichever suits you or exploring many and then choosing are perfectly acceptable by most standards if you're ready to know more about typography, or fonts. I say fonts with the word "fonts" in jest because in many ways that's all we are talking about, and talking about it at length is, well, fun for some. Enjoy!

*Bringhurst*

If you enter the world of typography from Western Canada like I did, among many other places that might have been, Robert Bringhurst would have been your entry point with his book The Elements of Typographic Style and perhaps also The Solid Form of Language. Bringhurst is framed as a poet, typographer, and author and I have fond memories of pulling his typography book off the shelf and feeling that I had pulled down a bible of sorts. In these books he goes into a kind of poetic complexity about the magic of type, which weaves itself into the form of his books, the paper choice, the elegant typographic illustrations on the cover, the infographics inside, the mathematical almost Tufte-esque charts, etc. Based on Quadra Island, my most recent news about him was that he was spending time turning oral languages into visual languages that previously only existed orally. Robert Bringhurst holds the Order of Canada.

*Spiekermann*

Erik Spiekermann is a Berlin-based German type designer, who spends time in the Bay Area, and is most known for his bestselling book Stop Stealing Sheep & Find Out How Type Works and his work on the font FF Meta. I recently interviewed him on my podcast Uniqueways and we spoke at length about his ability to tackle the most complex typographic problems, such as wayfinding and identity for an entire city or a city public transport wayfinding system. His outgoing personality combined with his no-nonsense ideas about rudimentary typography to make him an obvious choice to learn from early on. He coined a concept about how not to do letter spacing: "stealing sheep," a typographic technique for typesetting strings of text. This became part of his identity (or what you might call personal branding these days) and today's young graphic designers learnt about this growing up. He now runs a printing press revival studio in Berlin and invites guests in for typographic workshops.

*Lupton*

Ellen Lupton is an American contributor, not only in books but also in teaching. Lupton presents typography as well as things like grids in no-nonsense rhetoric. She makes it fun and not as typographic. Holding a long-standing Chair appointment at MICA (Maryland Institute College of Art) in Maryland, Lupton frequently publishes on the platform Skillshare, where she was an early contributor there. She is also currently focusing on Instagram Reels. If you aren't mixed in to the American vernacular you will still certainly come across her books in your early typographic education. Her hair and clothing style also compliment the ideas she is trying to convey: typographic ease and basics.

*Weingart*

If you were entering typography twenty or more years ago you certainly would have been aware of movements like postmodernism. Wolfgang Weingart was an active graphic designer during this movement. Graphic designers trying to make a difference in this movement published tomes: picture and concept books simply named "Typography" or something similar. I saw Weingart give a talk once as a teenager here in Vancouver and was taken by his straightforward approach to teaching typography. Those were the days before PowerPoint and he moved his typography on an analog projector in a way that made everyone in the packed auditorium shiver. Weingart made typographic simplicity a trend, if not a bit of an impossibility. Weingart's unmistakable orange and yellow Typography book cover, and the sheer weight of his tome, gave him a visual authority that was unforgettable and of that period. Strongly attached to postmodernism, Weingart had a certain attitude and expression that was synonymous with typographic auteurs of that time.

If the early internet was your entry point into typography, with mid '90s faces like Verdana and Georgia, Matthew Carter might have been your start. Known for his work on Microsoft Typography, his work on the Yale typeface, and his short appearance in the Helvetica film, Carter can be noted for having made letters in every way imaginable, starting with carving it out of lead for printing press type. On screen, Verdana, a "web font" that was a wide character sans serif and one of four fonts you could use on the web at one time, along with the serif Georgia, also one of those four fonts, would have been in your visual memory even if type wasn't your thing. Particularly in the typographic world, Carter has recorded the highest order of accomplishment, and is unforgettable in many ways.

*Gill*

Mainly known for his work on the British typeface Gill Sans, and his controversial personal life, Eric Gill probably could be an entry point of sorts. He has a rather small book widely published on the topic, and it would be unfair to exclude that if you are anywhere in the UK you will see his type everywhere. Bringing humanism and eccentricity of type into mainstream usage could perhaps be one of his notable accomplishments. Some characters of Gill Sans are noticed even from afar and if you are immediately attracted to that I would offer him as a starting point to this wacky world.

*Tam*

Keith Tam taught me typography at Emily Carr Institute of Art and Design here in Vancouver in the early 2000s. This was after graduating from the school as valedictorian and doing his masters in type design at University of Reading, a kind of typographic shrine masquerading as a department at a school. Tam spent time in the typographic world, at conferences and among typographic elite, shifting from place to place to teach typography, including professor appointments at Reading in the United Kingdom and Hong Kong Polytechnic. He currently runs the show at Hong Kong Design Institute in Hong Kong and has pioneered many of their offerings. I would be short-changing you not to mention his design of the typeface Arrival which is used almost exclusively on the wayfinding and signage systems at the University of Reading.

*Greiman*

April Greiman, noted in her Wikipedia entry as one of the first to use the computer to make art, was someone you might learn about through design history textbooks or Googling "notable typographers." Her unmistakable visual styles give her a place in the canon that cannot be surpassed. On the one hand in the realm of the Wolfgang Weingart but on the other hand a Zuzanna Licko, or perhaps Susan Kare, Greiman's work was and, at the same time, wasn't typography.

*Tufte*

Mostly known for his work at Yale and set of illustrative books including Envisioning Information and Beautiful Evidence, it is perhaps feasible that Edward Tufte is your first entry into typography, if you look at it in terms of symbols and icons and the visual language of an academic. Considered more of a stats guy, Tufte runs a very well-respected set of workshops that aren't typography but might be tugging at the heels of typography. It is strange that typography doesn't make it into academic vernacular where other things do, and this might be an instance of that happening. Many may argue that this doesn't belong here, but I'll include it for the purpose of adding a unique angle.

In my next piece I'll go into the future: the future and typography. It's a divergent shift away from the design history modality that I've been primarily writing in here. Through interviews and personal conversations you'll be happy to know that speaking with these individuals has unfurled what we all wonder about these days: what does your future look like?

*Where We Jump Forward To*

How does typography play a role in what's coming? There's no better way, in my mind, than to talk to the experts. Typographers seem to have an impetus to change their efforts, often quite radically, sometimes even abandoning their typographic modality, as if now is the time for that. So, let's jump in.

*Trochut*

I spoke with Alex Trochut during the early days of the mainstream AI evolution. He spoke at length about his 3-d or perhaps even 4-d type projects. It was very visual. But separate from that we got into his lineage, his family had been into typography and he was, in a way, born into it. We chatted about thoughts like: is there some sort of typographic DNA that he was gifted in his blood, and if this is true, what will that typographic DNA mean when visuals are all generated from AI? My first thought was about the richness of typographic history and how one might pull on that knowledge to create new knowledge, or in other words, plug the typographic academics into AI, teach the AI all this. It was tangential conversation to move it away from the visual. But when looking at the work of Trochut and his typographic posters and word marks and even processes, they were clearly on the outskirts of implementing his typographic DNA into this new world. Those of us not in the typographic realm might wonder how something so visual could mean anything at all in a world where visuals are created by AI. But as a person educated at a young age in typography it was as clear to me, we would be teaching typography to AI. If not now, soon.

*Porchez*

I spoke with Paris-based Jean Francois Porchez around the time I was in Paris for a conference and he responded to our conversation with a typographic poster that was, in my eyes, very postmodern, or perhaps could be assumed to be of some Parisian aesthetic I was unaware of at the time. It was a white poster with red lettering and the typographic treatment changed on each new line. One might ask what was the purpose of such a thing in terms of legibility and readability. But what was clear to me was that this was a response to a new typographic knowledge and way of doing things. At least in terms of subconscious work of a typographer, this was a sign of the future.

*Bantjes*

Marian Bantjes and I spoke over audio from her home on Bowen Island, a ferry ride from Vancouver. She seemed to be struggling financially but interestingly had opened a new online store to show off her AI collage work, seemingly targeting the art world. Anyone familiar with Bantjes will know her elaborate decorative ornamentation of typographic proclivity that catapulted her into fame, and, dare I say, typographic fame as well. So, I was obviously interested in the AI work as a direction of sorts into our potentially new AI / type world. One might argue Bantjes saw the AI age as a time to abandon typography, especially if looking at this AI collage work and its sparseness of typography. But I wanted to dig deeper, as clearly it had to segue between typographic ornamentation and AI collage, and I would extend the assumption to say that typography might reappear in this work. The question of what it means to be in this middle stage that is not quite typography and not quite AI perhaps points to where we are in this new world. It's a kind of in-between place where we can only guess what the future actually looks like, even when looking directly at what's right in front of us. Still Bantjes seemed heavily invested in AI at this early point, and it was clearly going to be a step for her.

*Hoefler*

Jonathan Hoefler of typography.com fame (and typefaces like Knockout and Gotham), came later into our current AI world. Hoefler posted his efforts to social media. The posts were masterful creations of devices that did different things in an almost Industrial-Revolution-inspired push. He accompanied his visual creations with prose that proposed some imaginary / non-imaginary context for the visual 3-d pieces. With this typeface designer we saw a departure from typography aside from the default text type that social media platforms offer.

*Hische*

At the time of this writing, I'm scheduled to have a talk with Jessica Hische. Hische was early to the notable typographer scene with her lettering push, essentially bringing elegantly crisp custom lettering to the forefront of the typography dialogue, not just hers but everyone's. Rather than seeing an AI angle from her recently, we've seen a push towards brick-and-mortar efforts, as she has opened Jessica & Friends. It's a designer's paradise: a shop, a real shop, on her block in Oakland, California. Touting neighbours on her block in a gentrified have-a-good-day-shopping bubble, as well as encouraging visitors to come by and say hi in person, Hische is now doing something few people are doing right now, investing in the real world. From ampersand t-shirts to framed art prints, Hische appears to believe that there is still life in traditional typography and typographer aesthetics where many are abandoning it. It's a relief for me to see this.

*Maeda*

John Maeda only speaks tangentially about typography usually, almost as a nice-to-have. But it's clear in his SXSW slide decks and manicured YouTube feed, typography is important to him.

Recently taking on the role of VP of AI at Microsoft, Maeda has been instrumental in launching a kind of curious comical series about cooking with AI, where he bakes AI tutorials in an actual staged kitchen, often inviting friends into the feed to laugh alongside him. In all seriousness he seems to communicate that AI fundamentals taught in an accessible way are important for all of us right now – or maybe that's him under the Microsoft umbrella. Regardless, typography has left his palette at the moment.

*Millman*

If branding makes the cut into typographic dialogue, Debbie Millman has a voice. She is Chair of the Masters in Branding program at the School of Visual Arts in New York City, and is extremely active in participating in trends in the realm of producing artifacts, deliverables, and other ephemera. Her marriage to a rockstar writer, Roxane Gay, put her clearly in the middle of the design conversation. They have absolutely taken the stage, recently going on a podcast tour broadcasting live conversations for in-person audiences. Millman is also notable for her ability to convince friends to look at the future, but hers seems to be AI free.

So, in a break from typography for a moment, I spoke with a friend named Kris Krug recently about all this. We were both at a hackathon surrounded by hundreds of hackers at the University of British Columbia, seeing what young minds are making these days. I infer that we both didn't exactly know why we were there. Somewhat in jest I said "we all have to be at least halfway, when all this AI stuff hits the fan, don't we?" Krug, who is mostly, quite obviously, invested in AI, fanned out his stack of AI art prints for me. We laughed a bit and he continued to show me what he was doing, as if quite obviously stating for me "the future is right here, I printed it out on my bubble jet printer." We parted ways. I pondered the names I've presented here and asked myself: is he right? Who are we supposed to ask anyway? Who gets this stuff? Maybe the answer is in the question.

# 12

# UNIQUEWAYS

182 Lisa Strausfeld, Designer Apr 4, 2024

181 Jonathan Barnbrook, Graphic Designer Apr 4, 2024

180 Grant Gibson, Writer Apr 4, 2024

179 Jim William, Author Mar 31, 2024

178 Azmina Poddar, Chief Creative Officer Mar 28, 2024

177 Kevin Hawkins, Design Leader Mar 26, 2024

176 Alfredo Enciso, Graphic Designer Mar 26, 2024

175 Nigel Holmes, Graphic Designer Mar 21, 2024

174 Veronika Burian, Type Designer Mar 20, 2024

173 Don Norman, Legend Mar 17, 2024

172 John Higgins, VP ECD Mar 16, 2024

171 Nick Longo, Creative Executive Mar 14, 2024

170 SNASK Mar 14, 2024

169 Terea Sdralevich, Graphic Designer Mar 12, 2024

168 Sadie Red Wing, Graphic Designer Mar 6, 2024

167 Natalie Nixon, PHD, CEO Mar 5, 2024

166 Anthony Burrill, Graphic Artist Mar 4, 2024

165 David Lockie, Founder Feb 29, 2024

164 Kevin Poveda, Tattoo Artist Feb 29, 2024

163 Martina Flor, Lettering Artist Feb 29, 2024

162 Irene Pereyra, Designer Feb 27, 2024

161 Jay Grandin, Co-Founder Feb 21, 2024

160 Josh Clark, UX Design Leader Feb 20, 2024

159 Bonnie Siegler, Graphic Designer Feb 19, 2024

158 April Greiman, Design Legend Feb 16, 2024

157 Aarron Walter, Author Feb 14, 2024

156 Lisa Congdon, Illustrator Feb 12, 2024

155 Elizabeth Tunstall, Academic Leader Feb 10, 2024 1

54 Jesi Carson, Interaction Designer Feb 8, 2024

153 Paul Boag, Digital Leader Feb 6, 2024

152 Jeff Gothelf, Author Feb 5, 2024

151 Jessica Hische, Lettering Artist Jan 30, 2024

150 Alison Rand, Experience Designer Jan 29, 2024

149 Rachel Botsman, Speaker and Author Jan 25, 2024

148 Alastair Simpson, VP Jan 23, 2024

147 Barry Katz, Talent Manager Jan 19, 2024

146 Andy Budd, Design Leader Jan 18 2024

145 Darren St Laurent, Realtor Jan 16, 2024

144 Greta Costioli, Art Director Jan 15, 2024

143 Chriselle Erguven, Student Jan 14, 2024

142 John E. McGlothlin, Adjunct Professor Jan 13, 2024

141 Kevin Buthane, Author Jan 12, 2024

140 Nick Finck, Design Leader Jan 11, 2024

139 Mike Kuz, Designer Jan10, 2024

138 Sarah Hyndman, Author and Speaker Jan 9, 2024

137 Chloe Kwok, TED Speaker Dec 20, 2023

136 Bruce Haden, Architect Dec 18, 2023

135 Pengmin Xu, Graphic Designer Dec 17, 2023

134 Marian Bantjes, Design Legend Nov 23, 2023

133 Jakob Trollbäck, Founder Nov 22, 2023

132 Eli Woolery, Lecturer Nov 20, 2023

131 Irene Vlachou, Type Designer Nov 20, 2023

130 Amy Lima, Product Designer Nov 15, 2023

129 Adam Urklinski, UX and HMI Designer Nov 11, 2023

128 Chloe Gottlieb, Executive Coach Nov 07, 2023

127 Vida Jurcic, Founding Partner Nov 05, 2023

126 Lili Gao, Consultant Oct 28, 2023

125 Lauren Von Dehsen, Experience Designer Oct 22, 2023

124 Glynis Tao, Business Consultant Oct 17, 2023

123 Ezgi Akcinar, PhD Oct 11, 2023

122 Ellen Lupton, Design Legend Oct 09, 2023

121 Nick Shinn, Typeface Designer Oct 03, 2023

120 Patrick Neeman, VP Oct 01, 2023

119 Kurt Whitelaw, Creative Director Sep 26, 2023

118 Sachin Chaves, Web Developer Sep 23, 2023

117 Mahyar Saeedi, Digital Media Designer Sep 20, 2023

116 Zaid Hisham, Architect Sep 13, 2023

115 Bruno Oro, Academic Sep 12, 2023

114 Miklos Philips, UX Leader Sep 11, 2023

113 Kris Krüg, Storyteller Sep 07, 2023

112 Abhi Murali, Storyteller Aug 31, 2023

111 Lasse Joergensen, Videographer Aug 30, 2023

110 Chris Do, Designer Aug 24, 2023

109 Karla Mercado, Designer Aug 24, 2023

108 Jean François Porchez, Type Designer Aug 21, 2023

107 Alexandra Sumina, UI/UX Designer Aug 10, 2023

106 Roman Wilhelm, Type Designer Aug 09, 2023

105 Christian Nicolay, Artist Jun 20, 2023

104 Pauline Lai, Designer Jun 08, 2023

103 Connor Lowe, Designer Jun 08, 2023

102 Gail Anderson, Design Legend Jun 05, 2023

101 Ria Chatterjee, Student May 25, 2023

100 John Bondoc, Industrial Designer May 24, 2023

99 Evan Lee, Artist May 11, 2023

98 Mark Simonson, Type Designer May 02, 2023

97 Jesse Showalter, Internet Personality Apr 20, 2023

96 Julie Van Oyen, Designer Apr 13, 2023

95 Bhumika Kalra, Student Apr 10, 2023

94 Steven Heller, Design Writer Mar 24, 2023

93 Richard Saul Wurman, Architect Mar 21, 2023

92 Timothy Goodman, Artist Mar 13, 2023

91 Jessica Helfand, Designer Mar 12, 2023

90 Flora Gordon, Ghost Designer Mar 10, 2023

89 Seb Curi, Artist Mar 02, 2023

88 Chavi Sethi & Noor Bains, Designers Feb 23, 2023

87 Lucy Hogg, Photo based Feb 09, 2023

86 Tara Rice, Creative Direction Feb 06, 2023

85 Peter Sobchak, Editor in Chief Feb 01, 2023

84 Todd Omotani, Senior VP Jan 14, 2023

83 Raymond Larabie, Type Designer Jan 11, 2023

82 Christopher Lee Sauve, Pop Artist Jan 11, 2023

81 Meg Stiven, Director Jan 07, 2023

80 Bisi Williams, Global Thought Leader Jan 04, 2023

79 Erik Spiekermann, Typography Legend Dec 20, 2022

78 Hasan Namir, Author Dec 18, 2022

77 Rebecca Baker-Grenier, Artist Dec 18, 2022

76 Lori Goldberg, Artist Dec 17, 2022

75 Carolina Becerra, Creative Dec 12, 2022

74 Tolu Garcia, Product Designer Dec 09, 2022

73 Jordan Girman, VP of User Experience Dec 07, 2022

72 Tori Zhao, Front-end Engineer Dec 06, 2022

71                                        Stephanie
Walter, Designer Dec 03, 2022

70 Terri Rodriguez-Hong, Designer Nov 29, 2022

69 Eric Lee, UX Designer Nov 28, 2022

68 Jarell Alvarez, Product Designer Nov 28, 2022

67 Joel Hladecek, Worldwide Creative Officer Nov 24, 2022

66 Claire Lee, Student Nov 19, 2022

65 Ken Skistimas, Manager Nov 18, 2022

64 Ally Mona, Bespoke Branding Co Nov 18, 2022

63 Thuyen Nguyen, Graphic Designer Nov 13, 2022

62 Kyle (Shâwinipinesì) St-Amour-Brennan, Entreprenuer Nov 11, 2022

61 GB Lee, Designer Nov 10, 2022

60 Priti Saini, Associate Director Nov 10, 2022

59 Jonathan Nodrick, Founder Nov 09, 2022

58 Robin Wood Stethem, Cofounder Nov 08, 2022

57 Rogier van der Heide, Lighting Designer Nov 08, 2022

56 Itamar Medeiros, Director of Design Nov 05, 2022

55 Trevor Jones, Educator Nov 04, 2022

54 Stevie Thuy Anh Nguyen, Designer Nov 02, 2022

53 Dr. Maria Lantin, Academic Oct 29, 2022

52 Eric Quint, Author Oct 28, 2022

51 Bruno Porto, Graphic Designer Oct 27, 2022

50 Sharad Khare, Digital Journalist Oct 27, 2022

49 Gagan Diesh, Sabbatical Oct 27, 2022

48 Rafael Puyana, Educator Oct 25, 2022

47 Debbie Millman, Chair Oct 18, 2022

46 Alex Trochut, Graphic Designer Oct 17, 2022

45 Paul Conder, Principal Oct 17, 2022

44 Mana Saei, Artist Oct 14, 2022

43 Kelly Small, Author Oct 13, 2022

42 Erik Olson, Artist Oct 12, 2022

41 Casey Hrynkow, Facilitator Oct 07, 2022

40 zeldasauce, Gamer Oct 03, 2022

39 Candy Wiyono, Senior Designer Oct 01, 2022

38 John Maeda, Chief Technology Officer Sep 29, 2022

37 Meena Kothandaraman, Experience Strategist Sep 29, 2022

36 Kushal Jadhav, Director Sep 25, 2022

35 Scott Bremner, M.A. Student Sep 24, 2022

34 Sughandi Luthra, Brand Protagonist Sep 23, 2022

33 Garth Mc Intosh, Environments Sep 17, 2022

32 Germaine Koh, Artist Sep 13, 2022

31 Arndt Klos, Communication Designer Sep 12, 2022

30 Jason DaSilva, Film Maker Sep 11, 2022

29 Hien Do, Accountant Sep 01, 2022

28 Dr. Am Johal, Director and Associate Aug 29, 2022

27 Dr. Ron Wakkary, Professor Aug 26, 2022

26 A. Laszlo Lazuer, Engineer Aug 26, 2022

25 Filip Zagorski, Graphic Designer Aug 25, 2022

24 Matea Kulic, Executive Director Aug 23, 2022

23 Dr. Ron Burnett, Order of Canada Aug 22, 2022

22 Yasaman Hoorfar, Fashion Designer Aug 21, 2022

21 Scott Mallory Jr., Artist Aug 20, 2022

20 Sugandhi Luthra, Brand Protagonist Aug 20, 2022

19 Sonny Assu, Artist Aug 18, 2022

18 Merunisha Moonilal, Lecturer Aug 18, 2022

17 Dan Segal, Associate Principal, UX / CX Aug 12, 2022

16 Izabela Sroka, Art Director Aug 10, 2022

15 Dr. Marco Bevolo, Adjunct Professor Aug 10, 2022

14 Angela Fama, Artist Aug 08, 2022

13 Dr. Philippe Pasquier, Professor Aug 08, 2022

12 Jo Wong and Dan Szuc, Co-founders Aug 06, 2022

11 Paresh Choudhury, Professor Aug 04, 2022

10 Sneha Rai, Flight Attendant Nov 26, 2023 (republished)

09 Katrina Heschel, UX Researcher Nov 26, 2023 (republished)

08 Michael Peter, UX Researcher Nov 26, 2023 (republished)

07 Keith Tam, Academic Nov 26, 2023 (republished)

06 Alan Jones, Curious Human Nov 26, 2023 (republished)

05 Nicole Ho-Sang, Personal Coach Nov 26, 2023 (republished)

04 Dr.  Garnet Hertz, Canada Research Chair Nov 26, 2023 (republished)

03 Mahyar Saeedi, Podcast Host Nov 26, 2023 (republished)

02 Srushti Kulkarni, UI/UX Designer Nov 26, 2023 (republished)

01 Natasa Razak, Interior Architect Nov 26, 2023 (republished)

# About the Author

Thomas Girard (born 30 December, 1980 in Vancouver, Canada) is a Canadian scholar. Girard was accepted to attend University of Oxford in lectures equivalent to graduate coursework. Girard has received several Emerging Scholar awards, first at the Design Principles and Practices conference in Barcelona, Spain at the prestigious ELISAVA. At Emily Carr University of Art and Design he received his second Emerging Scholar award. Other awards include RBC Emerging Scholar, Royal Bank of Canada Foundation. For 2021, he has been awarded an Emerging Scholar award from the New Directions in the Humanities conference in Madrid, Spain.

**You can connect with me on:**

- http://www.thomaskgirard.com
- http://www.twitter.com/onthomas_tweet

# Also by Thomas Girard

EMERGING SCHOLAR: GRATITUDE OF AN AWARD RECIPIENT

EMERGING SCHOLAR: GRATITUDE OF AN AWARD RECIPIENT SECOND EDITION

EMERGING SCHOLAR & OXFORD

EMERGING SCHOLAR & TED

EMERGING SCHOLAR: ASSISTANT PROFESSOR TENURE-TRACK.

EMERGING SCHOLAR: LECTURE AT THE SORBONNE

EMERGING SCHOLAR & ASSOCIATE DEAN OFFER

EMERGING SCHOLAR & THE OXFORD CENTRE

LIFE OR DEATH TYPOGRAPHY

EMERGING SCHOLAR & PARIS